To A.

May God bless
you as you read
this book.

Ken

ENGAGING THE CULTURE:

Why Sharing Your Faith Is No Longer an Option

Ken Dew

Engaging The Culture:
Why Sharing Your Faith Is No Longer an Option
Author: Ken Dew

While the author has made every effort to provide accurate Internet addresses at the time of publication, neither the publisher nor the author assumes any responsibility for errors or for changes that occur after publication.

Copyright © 2018 by Ken Dew www.KenDewResources.com
ISBN: 978-0-9835120-7-3
Library of Congress Control Number: 2018939608
Design & Layout by: Douglas DoNascimento
Published by: Briggs & Schuster
        BSA.IM

Printed in the United States of America

Dedication

This book is dedicated to my beautiful wife
of twenty-eight years, Renee,
to my four amazing children,
Rebecca, Benjamin, Rachael and Abigail,
and to my selfless parents,
Henry "Hank" and Shirley Dew.

Engaging the Culture:

Why Sharing Your Faith is No Longer an Option

"I have known Ken for many years. It has been a privilege to see him excel as a church planter, disciple maker, evangelist, and more importantly, as a husband and father. He has developed amazing Every Nation leaders who are serving all over the world.

"It can sometimes be intimidating to engage non-Christians in conversations about the gospel. But in Matthew 28:19, Jesus calls us to 'make disciples of all nations.' I hope this book equips and inspires you to engage your culture with the gospel to make disciples of all nations."

Steve Murrell
President, Every Nation Churches & Ministries
Author of *WikiChurch* and *100 Years From Now*
Founding Pastor of Victory Manila, Philippines

"Ps. Ken Dew analyses the spiritual battle that every Christian must face, identifying the nature and aspects of this confrontation; employing military terms that characterize this 'engagement' which necessarily occurs on many fronts. Ken emphasizes that well-armed Christians must today leave the comfort and isolation of the church, to pro-actively confront the skeptics, unbelievers and deceived in the larger community with the Truth and saving grace of the Gospel. *Engaging the Culture* thus details the 'rules of engagement,' while providing practical weapons, battle plans, strategies and tactics that ensure that the Christian militia is equipped with a successful 'modus operandi' that will glorify Jesus and reclaim the world for God."

Jeannie Mok OAM
Senior Minister and Founding Pastor of International City Church
Brisbane, Australia

"Ken has been a lifelong friend and partner in the gospel. He is a shining example of someone sold out to the cause of Christ. His integrity and faithfulness have made his ministry extremely fruitful.

"His book, *Engaging the Culture,* will make an impact on those who read it."

Dr. Rice Broocks
Co-founder of Every Nation
Author of *God's Not Dead* and *The Human Right*

"Ken Dew is a warrior. He engages darkness at every level and succeeds in defending the faith. I thank God for this book. *Engaging the Culture* does just what the title states. It engages, exposes and defeats the weak and baseless arguments coming at us in our culture every day. Read it, soak it in and successfully and strategically engage your culture on behalf of Jesus."

Dr. Jeff Voth
Professor of Leadership and Spiritual Formation
Oral Roberts University
Author of *CaveTime* and *Defending the Feminine Heart*
Pastor of Church 3434 Tulsa, Oklahoma

"Ken has given us a masterful approach and guide to fulfill the Great Commission. Having known Ken for over 20 years, he is a great example of living in and walking out the rules of engagement. His life and this book have greatly encouraged me and presented a fresh challenge to my life."

Sam Webb
Asia Leadership Team
Every Nation Ministries

"Most Christians talk about engaging our culture with the Gospel. Some Christians pray about engaging our culture with the Gospel. A rare few take action engaging our culture with the Gospel. Ken Dew is one of those rare men of action who really does what he says and prays."

Pastor Dave Polus
Every Nation City Church
Van Nuys, California

"Glad to see the book! It is well written and researched using a biblical mandate. *Engaging the Culture* calls for every Christian to proactively share the Faith and thereby confront the Worldviews that are so destructive of civilization and the value of human life. Sharing the Faith is an essential character of the Christian; this book provides both the mandate and the means for evangelization."

James B. Shelton, PhD
Professor of New Testament
College of Theology and Ministry
Oral Roberts University

Table of Contents

Acknowledgements

Without the help of many amazing friends and colleagues, this book quite simply would not have happened. To all these individuals, I am deeply indebted.

Firstly, I would like to thank my beautiful wife, Renee for the long hours of editing, wise advice, and love she has shown me through the completion of this book. This project would not have been possible without her loving encouragement and diligent help. Secondly, I would like to thank my eldest daughter Rebecca, who has contributed days of painstaking effort in editing, formatting and proofreading this manuscript. It was wonderful to have ready recourse to an English major and PhD while writing this book. I would also like to thank Benjamin, the son of my right hand, and my younger two amazing daughters, Rachael and Abigail, for their constant support and prayers, inspiring me to finish strong.

To Pastor Danny and Diane McDaniel and the staff of Bethel Dallas Church, thank you for being so supportive in covering this project in prayer. The McDaniels are two of the most honorable and generous people I have ever met. I also owe a world of gratitude to the following people for their friendships and prayers: Pastor Norman Nakanishi, Pastor Sam and Nancy Webb, Coach John Rohrer, Pastor Dave Polus, Pastor Kevin York, Pastor Steve Murrell, Dr. Leo and Pat Lawson, Pastor Jim Laffoon, Pastor David Houston, as well as, my long-time friends Jim and Laura Frazier. A special note of appreciation to my dear friends in the

South Pacific, especially Dr. Adam and Sandra Claasen who were instrumental partners in advancing God's Kingdom in Oceania.

Thank you, Leilani Haywood, for helping me in a pinch with the finishing touches of this project. I am deeply grateful for your encouragement and friendship that have brought this book to completion. I would also like to express my sincere gratitude to Mary Peterson who blessed me with her composition and editing skills, and Bill Jones who has patiently assisted me in the digital jungle of the IT world. Thank you, Douglas DoNascimento, my dear Brazilian friend and publishing agent for your tireless work and saint-like patience in helping me complete this project.

I would particularly like to acknowledge my lifelong friend Rice Broocks for obeying the Great Commission, coming to my campus at Tennessee Tech and preaching the gospel to me years ago, literally changing my life and destiny. Thank you.

Most of all, I would like to thank my Lord, Jesus Christ, who apprehended my heart thirty-seven years ago and gave my life definition as a part of fulfilling the Great Commission worldwide. May this book be a means of blessing those who have chosen to take part in His divine mission.

To God be the glory!

Foreword

We live in an age of blinding unprecedented change and massive cultural corrosion. In a world lacking the center of a Godly soul, there is nothing like this kind of book that brings us back to the unchanging gospel of Jesus Christ.

Ken Dew writes about the gospel not as an author but as a lifetime preacher, pastor, evangelist, apologist, teacher and activator of it in various nations of the earth, resulting in abundant fruit that not only speaks but shouts for itself. *Engaging the Culture* is enlarging and compelling, but most importantly it equips everyone from all walks of life with the working knowledge of how to engage a world with the only truth that can transform lives and change the societies who cradle them.

Read on and you will find clarity, be moved by the cause, draw closer to Christ, and gain a newfound confidence for what truly is a great mission. At a time when many treat the Great Commission as the great suggestion, we are lovingly reminded that one day we will give account for our response to engage bold strategic evangelism in a grand battle for eternal destinies.

The time is short, Christ could soon be coming and there is a heavenly audience from ages past urging us on: "Therefore, since we have so great a cloud of witnesses surrounding us, let us also lay aside every encumbrance, and the sin which so easily entangles us, and let us run with endurance the race that is set before us, fixing our eyes on Jesus, the author and perfecter of faith, who for the joy set before Him endured the cross, despising the shame, and has sat down at the right hand of the throne of God" (Hebrews 12:1-2).

So let us run with endurance in order that we may fight to the finish. *Engaging the Culture* not only confronts us spiritually with the cross but also equips us practically for its cause. Jesus started it; Paul and subsequent generations continued it, and it is now left to us to finish it. Read and engage. In God's eyes, sharing our faith has never been, nor shall ever be just an option. One day we will stand before God for our generation. With that in mind, let us go forward together.

Norman Nakanishi
Founder and Senior Pastor
Grace Bible Church Pearlside, Hawaii
Every Nation Ministries
North American Leadership Team

Introduction

There is no greater discovery than seeing God as the
author of your destiny.

- Ravi Zacharias[1]

The date was June 10th, 2014. I wiped the moisture from my
eyes as I boarded the plane heading back to the U.S. My wife, Renee
and I had served on the mission field planting churches in the South
Pacific for the last fourteen years. The faces of all the beautiful people
flooded through my mind as the plane taxied down the runway. They
had been a significant part of our lives, each one of them dramatically
changed by the gospel message.

Raising our four children in New Zealand and Australia was an
amazing experience. As a result of this decision to move to the South
Pacific, our lives had taken a turn that guaranteed that we would never
be the same again.

Our family had literally moved to the other side of the planet, far
away from the America that felt familiar and secure. When people asked
us why we moved to the South Pacific, all I could do was laugh and refer
them to the verse in Acts 1:8: "And you shall be My witnesses . . . even to
the remotest parts of the earth."

By God's grace, our family embarked on a daring adventure
that not only changed our lives, but impacted and transformed those
around us along the way. During that fourteen-year season, we had planted churches, established campuses ministries, started Bible schools and

raised up pastors, evangelists and ministry leaders. Now we were leaving the "land down under" and coming back to the United States.

God Makes All Things Possible

I learned early on in my Christian life that with God, not only are all things possible; possibilities are endless. I still remember attending a campus conference in Atlanta, Georgia, as a new believer thirty years ago. There were Christian students from all over the southeastern part of the country including Auburn University, the University of Georgia, the University of Tennessee, Georgia Tech University, the University of Florida and the University of Alabama.

At this conference there was also a fiery preacher speaking about global evangelism. He made a very profound statement that challenged me to take action. He said, "All you need is a Bible and a passport to reach the world!"

I considered that for a moment. *All I need is a Bible and a passport to reach the world!* Well, I already had a Bible. Now, all I needed was a passport.

I had never dreamed of going to a foreign country before, or of preaching the gospel there. At this point in my life, I was in my early twenties, and I had only travelled to about a dozen states. I am sad to say that at the time visiting Disney World in Orlando, Florida, or Six Flags in Atlanta, Georgia was about as big as my vision was. As I continue to grow as a Christian, however, I discover that God has a much bigger plan for His children. I soon realized that the mission field we are called to reach is worldwide.

As Christians we can become myopic and self-absorbed. I am convinced that God did not save us just to give us personal peace, affluence and security in this life.

There are, of course, many blessings and benefits granted to God's people in the here and now. We don't wait to start experiencing His presence and partaking of God's goodness until the sweet by and by. But if we as believers will be open and available to heed God's word and to take risks, God will use us as vehicles to transmit His message to the nations. Our Christian faith is not for our benefit alone. It is not just about our comfort and convenience. The faith we possess is to be contended for. It is for us as individuals, for families, and for future generations.

So, what happened? I finally *did* get my passport. And in the summer of '86 I took my first missions trip to the Philippines, a trip that changed my view about spreading the gospel forever.

Since then, I have had the tremendous privilege of meeting many unique people groups and living in exotic, beautiful lands. In our churches in Oceania there are Polynesian people from Samoa, Tonga, Papua New Guinea, the Cook Islands and Fiji. We have had church members from Australia, England, Spain, Greece, the Philippines, India, South Africa, Hong Kong, Malaysia, Singapore, and more. You get the picture.

The nations of the world were present at our doorstep, living in our cities, shopping in our malls, and attending our schools. At first it seemed very odd encountering all of these cultures. Getting to know and live among these diverse people groups in the South Pacific became a great joy to my wife, Renee and me.

Eventually, the cultural differences seemed to disappear. We found that we shared much in common. The beautiful spirit and sincere faith of these people melted our hearts. Just like me, all these people who came from various countries, tribes and cultures intuitively knew that there must be a deeper purpose for their lives.

We were able to introduce these people to the Creator of the universe, who was responsible for putting them in this world in the first place. We were able to share that the one thing that is universally common to all people is their dire need to know God and be reconciled back to Him. This is of course the reason we preach the gospel.

Jesus commanded His followers to take this gospel to the whole world (Mark 16:15). The overwhelming implication of Jesus' words is that the whole world, all people groups and all nations, need to hear the good news, the gospel.

As an evangelist, pastor and church-planter, my primary desire for writing this book is to help motivate and inspire believers to take their Christian faith outside the confines of their church circles. You may not know how to do that just yet. You may think that there are many different ways to bring God glory and help advance His Kingdom here on earth. And, in fact, there are, but they all involve accepting, loving and influencing other people. As Christians we all want to honor Jesus with our lives and introduce other people to Him. The promise made in Scripture is clear: "But a life lived loving God bears lasting fruit, for the one who is truly wise wins souls" (Proverbs 11:30 TPT).

If you and I want to attain godly wisdom and enjoy a productive life, we will need to be ready to reach people with the gospel. In fact, one of Jesus' main objectives during His earthly ministry was to "seek and save that which was lost" (Luke 19:10). In other words, to borrow a Christian cliché, we exist to make the name of Jesus famous.

One of my goals in writing this book is to encourage all Christians to realize that God is fully able to take anyone from any walk of life and empower that person to reach others with His truth. I am so grateful to God for allowing me to take part in the adventure of taking the gospel around the world. My life, my marriage, and my family have been truly blessed and enriched by participating in the Great Commission.

So, there I was on that plane, headed back to the United States with my family after fourteen years on the mission field.

Suddenly, I was interrupted in my reminiscing by one thought: *What if Renee and I had not said "Yes" to God?* What if we had not made ourselves available for Him to work through us to reach the lost? What if we had never gone on the mission field? Many of these people would never have been reached. None of these churches would have been planted. Our children would have missed out on the amazing cross-cultural experiences and international opportunities. But most of all, God would not have received the glory He deserved.

After spending over a decade on the foreign mission field, my family and I had been exposed to many different cultures and exhilarating experiences that I could never even have dreamed of growing up in America. God had bigger plans! As believers, there is no limit to what God can do if we are committed to His purposes.

Signs of the Times

On the surface America appears to be strong and growing, still the military protector of much of the free world and a bastion of liberty for all. Our presidents still publicly pray and host annual celebrations in recognition of the role of faith in our nation. Christian television programming abounds, and mega churches dot the landscape. Our dollar bill is still emblazoned with the slogan "In God We Trust." But, as we look a bit deeper into our affairs, a disturbing reality becomes apparent. Many Americans are trusting in the wrong currency, a currency of personal peace and material affluence.

The kind of indecent behavior, which was shunned and unthinkable a generation ago, is now celebrated under the banner of tolerance and diversity. Moral decay has gradually crept in, as people become complacent and adopt an anemic form of Christianity.

Author Jacques Barzum defines *decadence* as *adapting to culture* and defines *revolution* as *forcing culture to adapt.*[2] Unfortunately, it appears Western Christianity has drifted from revolution to decadence the last few decades.

America seems adrift in a sea of secularism, untethered from her past and forgetful of her Judeo-Christian foundations.

We are in a time in human history when morality, truth, western values and Christianity are under assault. The Christian faith is being targeted as though there were a large bulls eye on its back. Often believers and their views are trivialized and dismissed on a regular basis in the name of tolerance and political correctness. The current secular environment is increasingly hostile to Christian morality and biblical truth. With these social and cultural challenges pressing the Christian Church, we must turn to the hope of redemption found only in the good news of Jesus Christ.

Ironically, this growing cultural opposition has positioned the truth of the gospel to come more clearly into focus. It has also provided amazing opportunities for Christians to engage and speak this truth in love.

The Bible declares, "but where sin increased, grace abounded all the more" (Romans 5:20). *What a magnificent promise!* I believe God's grace is more than sufficient for Christians to engage their cultures with the gospel message to redeem what's broken and lost. There has never been a more opportune time for the Church to stand up and boldly contend for the Christian faith.

Contenders for the Faith

The Letter of Jude was written to encourage the first century Christians to *contend* for their faith. "Beloved, while I was making every effort to write you about our common salvation, I felt the necessity to write to you appealing that you *contend earnestly for the faith* which was once and for all handed down to the saints" (Jude 3, emphasis mine). The challenge at hand is to stand our ground and accept the task of preaching the gospel, exhorting people everywhere to "be saved from this perverse generation" (Acts 2:40).

Jude uses the Greek word *epagonizomai* in this verse, which translates into English as the compound verb "earnestly contend." The Greek word here literally means *to compete in an athletic contest, to fight, struggle and strive.* It is clear from Jude's exhortation that we as Christians are meant to fight for, to ruthlessly defend our faith at all costs.[3]

In other words, believers had better get ready. This battle is real, and the fight is so serious that it demands our full engagement. Just like in Jude's time, believers today must realize that contending for our faith is not necessarily a defensive measure. Although at times we are called to defend our faith and to offer a reason for the hope that is in us, at times contending for our faith is a *proactive* and *deliberate* act.

We are meant to be intentional, not hesitant but fearless with our evangelistic efforts. Contending for the faith means that believers must preach the message with passion and clarity.

The classic definition for *preaching* is *the communication of divine truth through human personality.*[4] For some reason God always chooses human beings as instruments for spreading the gospel throughout the earth.

I am reminded of Cornelius' vision in the Book of Acts. Scripture states that Cornelius was a devout man who feared the Lord. While he was praying, Cornelius saw a vision of an angel of God. The angel proceeded to tell Cornelius to dispatch his servants to the city of Joppa and to bring back a man Simon, called Peter. The servants went to Joppa to retrieve Peter as directed. Then Peter traveled back to meet Cornelius and preached the gospel to his entire household (Act 10:1-42).

But why did God need Simon Peter to deliver His message to Cornelius' household anyway? Why didn't the angel just preach the gospel to Cornelius himself? It seems to me that supernatural messengers such as an angelic being would do a much better job. But Romans 10:14 is quite clear: "How will they hear without a preacher?" God's divine plan includes imperfect people to communicate His gospel to the ends of the earth.

During my personal fight of faith, I have been spiritually knocked down, beaten up, dazed, bruised, overjoyed, depressed, confused and encouraged. There have even been times when the bell rang in the wrestling ring of ministry, that I was so exhausted I didn't want to come out of my corner for the next round. I've also had glorious moments when I was having so much fun seeing God's enemies pushed back and defeated and souls being saved, that I did not want to sit down when the round was over!

Through all the victories and hardships, both the valleys and the mountaintops, God has always been faithful to sustain and encourage me. That's exactly why Paul told Timothy to "fight the good fight of faith" (1 Timothy 6:12). It is a *good* fight because the Lord has already secured the victory for us!

With this in mind, I hope to bring some light on overcoming through sharing the challenges we faced, and the many victories that my family and I have experienced during our years of ministry. I hope that these experiences are a blessing to you, and inspire you to allow God to use you as His messenger.

The gospel of Jesus Christ is the greatest news ever told. When believed, it is the one truth that can transform a life, a city or an entire nation. As followers of Jesus, we must do all we can to get the message out by engaging our culture with the truth: Who Jesus is and what He has done through His life, atoning death and resurrection.

As Matthew 28:19-20 commands, "Go therefore and make disciples of all the nations, baptizing them in the name of the Father and the Son and the Holy Spirit, teaching them to observe all that I commanded you; and lo, I am with you always, even to the end of the age." This is what Christians and theologians commonly refer to as *the Great Commission*. This Great Commission was not just a good idea or an afterthought. These were the last words Jesus spoke to His disciples, a command to be implemented in their approach to living their daily lives. We too must be intentional in overcoming every excuse if we are to make ourselves available to be used by God.

No Longer an Option

When you read the title of this book, *Engaging the Culture: Why Sharing Your Faith is No Longer an Option*, you might have been thinking that sharing your faith was at some time or another optional. Hopefully, by the end of this book you will see that sharing your faith is not an option, and never has been.

The Great Commission may seem challenging to the average person. How can God use ordinary people like you and me to spread His truth to a world that doesn't even know it needs to hear it? Much of American culture seems to be sliding into a self-indulgent haze, spiritually sick while oblivious to its own illness. But despite the modern challenges to our faith, we are to be confident in the Mighty One who resides within us as believers.

If Christians are to be agents of change, we've got to overcome the real and perceived barriers to talking with people who don't always agree with us. We must become comfortable and skilled at engaging people in public settings about God's ultimate plan for redemption.

Since becoming a Christian, I have always had a deep desire to be used by God in evangelism and to train believers to evangelize. God has graciously enabled my wife and I to identify and train many Christian leaders over the years. My goal for writing this book is to help motivate and release you, the reader, into a greater capacity for use in God's service.

That is why *Engaging the Culture* can help you reach the world around you. Together in this book we will:

- Examine the scriptural mandate given for all Christians to be ready to give a defense for the hope that is within them.
- Identify some of the basic challenges that most Christians face when trying to share the gospel.
- Communicate life lessons I have learned over the last thirty years both as an evangelist on the university campus and as a church planter.
- Develop evangelistic competence, the ability to present the gospel to unbelievers in a clear and winsome way and to disciple new believers to spiritual maturity.

After reading this book, I am convinced that you will feel more confident as a Christian about what you believe and why you believe it. You will know how to live in agreement with those beliefs, and you will know how to love and influence those whose beliefs are contrary to your own.

Engaging the Culture will help you identify the common challenges to sharing your faith and equip you to be ready to answer the skeptic or Bible critic with confidence, clarity and compassion.

My prayer is that you will be encouraged to begin the journey to embrace God's heart and His command to reach a lost and broken world with Christ. His plan of redemption is truly great. God is fully able to stir your passion for evangelism in whatever form it takes and allow you to feel the spiritual exhilaration and satisfaction of knowing that your life and words can alter someone's eternal destiny.

May the Lord bless you with confidence to embrace and act on the evangelistic principles presented in this book. Remember your greatest ability is your availability. Get ready to engage your culture and make your Christianity count.

CHAPTER ONE

What are the Rules of Engagement?

Rules of Engagement (ROE): As a military term, directives issued by an authority, specifying the circumstances and limitations under which ground, naval and air forces will engage in combat with the enemy.[5] In terms of Christian mission and the purposes of this book, directives issued by Jesus Christ to spread the gospel throughout the world.

In February 2015, I was invited to minister at a church in Los Angeles and speak at a men's conference. The night before the conference, I had the opportunity to meet one of the other guest speakers. He made an immediate impact on me because he had bravely served in the military as a Navy SEAL. Now, he works as a Hollywood stuntman.

I knew it was not a coincidence that I began writing this book at about the same time. Jeff, a devout Christian, retired from the Navy as a decorated war hero. That night he shared with us about some of his military exploits while he had served in the Middle East combat zone. I sat with scores of other men, mesmerized, listening to story after story of Jeff's military experiences.

At the end of the meeting, I asked Jeff to explain his perspective of what he thought the term Rules of Engagement (ROE) meant, both in a military setting and in a spiritual sense. I was so impressed with his definition that I have included it here:

> Spiritually speaking, the real enemy that we face on a daily basis has not changed his tactics since the moment of his first interaction in the Garden of Eden. He distracts, lies (which are often laced with truth) and misleads. Knowing his strategy is only part of the battle. Knowing which battles to fight is quite another factor.
>
> The enemy likes to "recon by fire" only because he is not omniscient, or omnipotent. He does not always know what you have been designed to do by God, or what mission you may currently be on. If you chose to engage the enemy's recon by fire, you could be fighting a fight that you do not need to engage, thus it is a distraction.
>
> Reconnaissance by fire does not mean firing blindly with the hopes of hitting something. It is a technique of firing into areas believed to contain the enemy in order to provoke them into returning fire or fleeing, at which time they can be engaged using more precise methods. The enemy's moves can often be anticipated, mainly because of the intelligence that is offered. The Word of God has the best battle plan, complete with the enemy's methodology, and it includes our Rules of Engagement as soldiers in the Kingdom of God.[6]

Building on Jeff's definition, I consider the word "engagement" or "engage" to best capture the Christian's mission of taking the message of who Christ is and what He has done to the world. Much of contemporary Christianity is focused on getting people to attend a church meeting or a Bible study. But in fact many believers know very little of what vibrant Christianity looks like outside of the church building or the theology classroom. Taking the gospel outside of the church and religious circles is an essential step to impact a lost and spiritually dark world.

There are, of course, several different meanings that we can take from the word *engagement*. *Engage* is a verb meaning *to encounter; to begin to fight; to attack in conflict.*[7] What becomes clear in all of these definitions is that the meaning of the word *engage* elicits a requirement for *intentional interaction*. Christ intentionally engaged us when He came to earth. My use of the term is designed to encourage people to come to grips with the task God has for them to do and get ready to take action.

The Battle Rages On

Scripture confirms that there exists an ongoing spiritual struggle between the Kingdom of God and the Kingdom of Darkness (Colossians 1:13). The Apostle Paul wrote to the Christian believers in the church at Ephesus, "For our struggle is not against flesh and blood, but against the rulers, against the powers, against the world forces of this darkness, against the spiritual forces of wickedness in heavenly places" (Ephesians 6:12). This means as Christians, we are meant to engage in battle on two fronts.

First, we are to put on our spiritual armor and enter into spiritual battle taking up "the full armor of God, so that you will be able to resist in the evil day" (Ephesians 6:13). We can engage in spiritual warfare in many ways. For example, through intercession and praise we can route the enemy (2 Chronicles 20:22) and release angelic aide to those who are harassed or perishing (Isaiah 44:26). Through our prayer and fasting, we can bring deliverance to others (Matthew 17:21), and through praying in the Spirit, we can pray according to God's divine will (Romans 8:26-27). Spiritual engagement, although not a physical battle of flesh and blood, is a very important part of addressing the culture with the gospel.

Secondly, Christians are to engage intentionally with non-Christians for the sake of exposing them to the message of Jesus Christ and

His saving grace. This is part of the Great Commission. It is not violent, in terms of what we normally understand as violent, but it can be confrontational to those who have never heard of Christ and, as a result, do not really know who He is. Paul, in the Book of Ephesians, exhorts the church to engage in spiritual warfare and asks them to pray for something very practical:

> *With all prayer and petition pray at all times in the Spirit, and with this in view, be on the alert with all perseverance and petition for all the saints.*

> - Ephesians 6:18

Again, in 2 Corinthians Paul writes:

> *For though we walk in the flesh, we do not war according to the flesh, for the weapons of our warfare are not of the flesh, but divinely powerful for the destruction of fortresses. We are destroying speculations and every lofty thing raised up against the knowledge of God, and we are taking every thought captive to the obedience of Christ.*

> - 2 Corinthians 10:3-5

I believe that Paul is not only speaking to the individuals in those churches to engage in spiritual warfare and harness their thoughts, but he is also exhorting us as believers today to address the speculations and lofty thoughts that are being raised up in our culture that are contrary to Christ and His Kingdom.

Until a person hears about who Christ is, he or she won't be able to respond to His love. Often I have found that it is the people who have never heard about God's love who are the most eager and curious to find out about it.

The biggest confrontation taking place is the conflict that occurs within the unbeliever's own soul. There is a battle going on for their souls and their eternal destiny. The Apostle Paul's letter to Timothy in the middle of the New Testament gives us a glimpse of the true nature of fallen humanity, and the motivation we have as Christians to share the gospel with others: "that they may come to their senses and escape from the snare of the devil, having been held captive by him to do his will" (2 Timothy 2:26).

In other words, many people are simply deceived. It is important to state that the problem with deception cannot be laid as being the fault of the truth or those who proclaim it. The real problem with deception is that those who are deceived don't realize they are! That is exactly why deception is so dangerous. Those who are deceived are oblivious to the deception.

Take the following example. People who suffer from anorexia are extremely underweight and physically unhealthy. But whenever they look at themselves in the mirror, they see and believe they are overweight based on a distorted image of reality and a legalistic desire for perfection. In short, they are deceived.

Deception blinds people to the true status of their condition. In most cases, people are not even aware of the spiritual warfare that rages on all around them. Their spiritual understanding is darkened. One of the worst manifestations of self-deceit is human pride. Pride is the unwillingness or inability to accept our own sin for what it really is: Rejection of the relationship with God that He designed and privileged mankind to walk in with Him. Many people are blinded by the Kingdom of Darkness, unable to recognize the Kingdom of Light. They are captivated by the carnal pursuits of their fallen natures, lost from the knowledge of the one Truth that could save them, if they only were willing to humble themselves to accept it.

Knowing that our battle is spiritual and that the presentation of the gospel requires our practical involvement, we cannot dismiss the real conflict that is taking place in the hearts and minds of men and women across the world. Eternal salvation is on the line.

In a military situation involving live combatants, the battle is physical, flesh and blood, life and death. It is either kill or be killed. The notion of physically eliminating the enemy and winning the war is the goal of any successful military campaign. But, in terms of the battle of the spirit realm, winning the hearts and souls of the opposition is our motive for engaging others. We do not want to destroy anyone. Instead, we share the desire of Jesus Christ to *see every soul saved* (2 Peter 3:9).

According to Scripture, all people are made in the image of God,[8] and everyone is worth saving, including those who deny the truth about God. Regardless of race, culture, education, background, beliefs or social status, all people have intrinsic God-given value because we bear the divine imprint of the God who made us (Genesis 1:26-27). Redemption is the promise of the hope that Christ has given *to those who believe.*

That is why, in this book, we will use the term Rules of Engagement not in a strictly military sense, but instead as a means of helping us identify the principles and outlook needed to become proactive emissaries of our faith and to engage with every culture in every nation. We are meant to *take* our faith to the front lines. So, for our discussion in this book, the term *engage* will be used to indicate *a sense of ongoing interaction on the part of Christians with other people who have not yet heard or accepted the gospel message.*

I have identified the following five rules of engagement.

> ➤ **Rule #1: Accept Your Mission.**
> ➤ **Rule #2: Clarify Your Message.**
> ➤ **Rule #3: Live Your Message.**
> ➤ **Rule #4: Speak with Confidence.**
> ➤ **Rule #5: Think and Act Strategically.**

For example, this past July my daughter Rebecca and I went to a ten-day seminar series in Seattle, Washington. The seminar provided advanced training on the subject of Intelligent Design. The conference was very informative, but also quite academically rigorous. When we got on the plane to head home, I was extremely tired and really wanted to catch a nap on the long flight back to Dallas. As I sat scrunched up between two other people, the man sitting in the aisle seat to my left started asking me questions about my visit to Seattle. With little or no enthusiasm, I told him about the nature of the conference and how we learned that the natural and biological sciences make belief in Intelligent Design quite reasonable. That may not have been the expressed goal of the conference, but it was what we took away from it.

At that point this guy started shooting me a barrage of questions, one after the other. *What about evolution? Hasn't science disproved the Bible? What about all the corruption in the Catholic Church? If God is so good, why does*

He allow evil in the world? I mean this dude was hitting me with questions, and they were rapid fire!

For the next two hours I spent my time on that plane speaking with this man, answering his questions as best I could. By the time we were getting ready to touch down in Dallas, he stopped and said, "You have answered all of my questions and given me a lot to think about. Thank you." He went on to say that he had been deeply hurt by the Catholic Church as a young man, and, as a result, didn't know if he could trust religion ever again. All I could do was tell him that I understood his position, and sympathized with his disappointment.

The church has hurt many people, and I am not immune to causing or receiving similar pain, either. I then asked him if I could pray for him. He agreed, and I prayed for Jesus to heal this man's mistrust and show him the truth regarding God's love.

Not only was I able to answer this man's questions regarding evil, along with some of the history of the Catholic Church and the debate surrounding evolution, but I was also able to tell him the truth about Jesus' life, death and resurrection. I gave him the full gospel message and prayed for him as we landed in Dallas.

He did not turn his life over to Jesus at that precise moment, but I knew that seeds of the truth had been planted in his heart. I may never see this man again, but this I know for sure: "God's word never returns void but will accomplish its purpose" (Isaiah 55:11). If we are going to engage the world, we must always be ready to give an answer for the hope that is within us.

Lay a Foundation

Everyone who comes to Me and hears My words and acts on them,
I will show you who he is like: he is like a man building a house,
who dug deep and laid a foundation on the rock; and when the flood
occurred, the torrent burst against that house and could not shake it,
because it had been well built.

- Luke 6:47-48

To present a clear gospel message and to lay a solid, theologically sound foundation, it is important to have a clear understanding of three truths: 1) the nature and character of God, 2) the true nature of humanity and 3) the reality of eternal judgment. Without first understanding the great dilemma of the chasm between God's holy character and mankind's fallen nature, we miss the true essence of what makes the gospel really good news.

1) The Nature and Character of God.

The Bible tells us that God is an all-powerful, eternal being who created all the plants, animals, people, planets, stars and galaxies in the universe. He caused all matter, energy and space to come into existence, along with all of the animal and plant life that exists on the face of the earth. The apex of God's creation was humanity. God created man and woman in His own image and likeness. God and the humans He created were in perfect fellowship, walking in intimate relationship with one another.

In the beginning God created the heavens and the earth. And the earth was formless and void, and darkness was over the surface of the deep, and Spirit of the God was moving over the surface of the waters. And God said let there be light; and there was light. And God saw the light, that it was good.

- Genesis 1:1-2

Then the Lord God formed man of dust from the ground and breathed into his nostrils the breath of life; and man became a living being.

- Genesis 2:7

Scripture clearly defines God's nature in the following ways:

God is All Powerful:	**Jeremiah 10:12**
God is All Knowing:	**Psalm 139:1-4**
God is Holy:	**Psalm 108:7**
God is Righteous:	**Romans 1:17**
God is Just:	**Deuteronomy 32:4**
God is Loving:	**1 John 4:8**
God is Faithful:	**Psalm 100:5**

To sum up God's nature, Scripture provides the essence of what makes God different from mankind. "Great and marvelous are Your works, Lord God Almighty; just and true are Your ways" (Revelations 15:3). And again: "Righteousness and justice are the foundation of Your throne; lovingkindness and truth go before You" (Psalm 89:14).

2) The True Nature of Humanity.

God created human beings in His image, holy, able to walk in perfect relationship and obedience with Him. God named the first man Adam and gave him a helpmate, woman, later named Eve. God's plan for Adam and Eve was for them to choose to walk daily in close relationship with Him. Unfortunately, Adam and Eve chose to disobey God. Through their disobedience, sin entered into the world, staining their nature, plunging all of humanity into sin. Sin is what separates humanity from God.

> *As it is written, "There is none righteous, not even one; there is none who understands, there is none who seeks for God; all have turned aside, together they have become useless; there is none who does good, there is not even one."*
>
> *- Romans 3:10-12*

> *Among them we too all formerly lived in the lusts of our flesh, indulging in the desires of the flesh and of the mind, and were by nature children of wrath, even as the rest.*
>
> *- Ephesians 2:3*

> *For while we were in the flesh, the sinful passions, which were aroused by the Law, were at work in the members of our body to bear fruit for death.*
>
> *- Romans 7:5*

3) The Reality of Eternal Judgment.

Because all humanity is born into sin, inheriting a fallen, carnal nature, all of humanity stands condemned in the light of God's perfect justice. Scripture is clear that all people must give an account for their actions.

For we must all appear before the judgment seat of Christ, so that each one may be recompensed for his deeds in the body, according to what he has done, whether good or bad.

- 2 Corinthians 5:10

Then He will also say to those on His left, 'Depart from Me, accursed ones, into the eternal fire which has been prepared for the devil and his angels.

- Matthew 25: 41

When the Lord Jesus will be revealed from heaven with His mighty angels in flaming fire, dealing out retribution to those who do not know God and to those who do not obey the gospel of our Lord Jesus. These will pay the penalty of eternal destruction, away from the presence of the Lord and from the glory of His power.

- 2 Thessalonians 1:7-9

As we can see, the true spiritual condition of humanity apart from God's mercy is very desperate. The need is urgent for the Christian church to rise up at this time. We must not lose our way or squander our moment in history. To be evangelistic in our faith is not to be part of an irrelevant religious subculture but to participate in one of the greatest adventures ever given by God. We get to participate in the life of the church and be stewards of God's redemptive message by taking the gospel to everyone who has ears to hear.

Power to be a Witness

The Book of Acts reveals an amazing promise to us: "But you will receive power when the Holy Spirit has come upon you; and you shall be My witnesses both in Jerusalem, and in all Judea and Samaria, and even to the remotest part of the earth" (Acts 1:8).

This power of the Holy Spirit was given to the disciples and early believers to help reconcile the lost crowds of humanity who were alienated from God by their sins. God's power to be witnesses is still available to believers today.

Are we as Christians convinced that God has commissioned and empowered us to engage in propagating the gospel to the lost? Or do we think that we can avoid responsibility simply by isolating ourselves and creating some sort of false sense of peace? For many believers, sadly, the question remains unspoken and unanswered.

From where I stand, I believe there are three options set before us.

1. **Isolation:** Isolating ourselves from engaging the lost and retreating into our holy huddles and religious activities.
2. **Peace Treaty:** Making a peace treaty with the world by trying our best to accommodate, tolerate and understand them and be tolerated and understood by them.

OR

3. **Engagement:** Engaging the world with the radical, redemptive claims of the gospel of Jesus Christ and thereby extending the Kingdom of God's amazing power in and through our lives and relationships.

Have you found yourself in a convenient form of *isolation* or maybe resigned yourself to an informal *peace treaty* with the lost? It's time to do some honest self-evaluation. It is not too late to engage the world around you. Remember, refusing to share your faith can no longer be an option.

CHAPTER TWO

The Divine Agenda

Agenda: A plan of things to be done or problems to be addressed; the underlying intentions or motives of a particular person or group.[9]

The church and its gospel throw into question the agenda of the world - all the agendas of the world - and open the world to possibilities of which it has never dared to dream. When the church dares to be different, it models for the world what God calls the world to become.

- Richard John Neuhaus[10]

God has a divine agenda for each one of us. However, many people today are consuming their time with seeking pleasure, possessions or status rather than in spending their lives doing something that is meaningful or eternal.

God's agenda might not appeal to us as the most pleasurable at first. The advertising industry spends billions of dollars every year creating a perceived need for people to purchase something they "just can't live without." We are often led to purchase something by imagining how it will make us feel, and make us obtain happiness.

The average person on the street seldom stops to think about Madison Avenue's marketing methods or motivations. As consumers, we might just want to stop and ask ourselves the question: Why are these companies marketing their products to us? What's in it for them? Do they really care about us? The answer should be obvious: Companies and their marketers have an agenda to sell us something, not because they want our happiness necessarily, but because they want our money.

It is not just the telemarketer or the stereotypical car salesman that has a hidden agenda. We all do. We may not even be in touch with what our deepest motives are for doing the things we do. Some of our motivations are honorable and may be beneficial to others. Conversely, some of our agendas may also be self-serving and petty. Personal happiness is the driving force behind most of the things we do or buy. One thing is certain: We all operate with ulterior motives and agendas.

I still remember a rather humorous incident my wife Renee had with one of our children. At the time, our youngest daughter Abigail was around three years old. Abigail was playing with a fragile, glass ornament. If dropped, it would have easily broken.

Renee told Abigail that she was not to touch or play with that ornament. Shortly after, Abigail asked her mother if she would please leave the room. Trying not to reveal her amazement at her child's bold request, Renee asked, "Why do you want me to leave the room, Abigail?" The response, though cute, was quite revealing: "I don't want you to see what I am doing."

Ask any athlete or competitor and they will understand that *if you get rid of the referee, then there is no violation.* If there is no one there to witness a violation of the law, then for all practical purposes, no law was broken! Although such an agenda may seem "adorable" coming from a three-year-old child, we are too aware of how undesirable such a motivation could become, if left unchecked.

Young Abigail's motivation to get her mother to leave the room was driven by her not-so-hidden agenda to disobey her mother's directive. From the youngest to the oldest, everyone has an agenda. Abigail's request was the oldest trick in the book.

We Had an Agenda

When we moved to Auckland, New Zealand as missionaries, one of our main strategies for ministry was to reach the local community in tandem with reaching out to university and high school campuses in the city. We had an agenda! We knew the need and intentionally targeted these segments of this new mission field.

God gave us immediate success on both fronts. We not only saw many families in the community start attending our church, but we also saw hundreds of university students come to Christ and be added to our ministry.

Many institutions and organizations develop what they call a *mission statement*. The mission statement is a prime directive that gives the organization or individual identity, authority and purpose. It sets the person apart for a specific purpose, and unites the organization towards the attainment of a common goal.

All believers have a mission to accomplish. You and I must find our *own personal mission field*. Our mission is called the *Great Commission*, and it is found in Matthew chapter 28. The task of propagating the gospel is not meant to be optional for the believer, a leftover assignment to be completed whenever all his or her other homework is done. It is among the Christian's *core values*. As believers, the challenge is not only to understand God's agenda but also to accept His mission.

God has sovereignly redeemed us for the purpose of making His name known and glorifying His name in all the earth. The missional Christian should therefore see all things through the lens of the gospel.

Jesus invites all of His followers to be agents of the Kingdom's advancement on earth. God's agenda will be evident when believers demonstrate a love for lost people and a commitment to make God's agenda their own.

➢ Rule #1: Accept Your Mission.

From the very beginning of our departure from America to our landing in New Zealand, we had a very clear mission. We wanted to plant churches and reach university students with the gospel. Our reasons for moving to Auckland were upfront and visible, clear to anyone who asked. As missionaries, we wanted to personally witness to the truth that had changed our lives. As Christians, we offered the world around us a new way of life.

Theologian Calvin Miller describes missions in this way:

> Missionaries are called to pay attention to the world. They are salespersons in a world of consumers who want to buy a different destiny - and that is exactly what the world is seeking - selling the kingdom should be easy and the transaction customary.[11]

Without a doubt, people have a reason for the things they do and for the things they desire. This is why in New Zealand we used a variety of evangelistic methods to communicate the gospel message to the city. Some of the tools we used were multimedia presentations on important topics like "Love, Sex and Dating," "Shadows of the Supernatural" and "Evolution: A Theory in Crisis." These seminars were fast-paced and contained hard-hitting video footage exposing spiritual deception and debunking false philosophies, while at the same time introducing biblical truths to the audience.

Hundreds of students attended these seminars, and many students were won to Christ. Our outreach methods also utilized a little booklet known as "The Two Question Test." This little evangelistic survey was developed by Francis Anfuso and Christian Equippers International, and proved to be a very effective tool in starting a spiritual conversation with unbelievers.

We also took care to explain the Christian faith intelligently, not just as a religious concept but also as a fundamental lifestyle change. Personal discipleship was what made the difference in establishing these new believers into the faith. *Discipleship* is *the process by which a new believer is helped to grow in their new relationship with Jesus and get established in the Christian faith, in the Word of God and in the Church (Spiritual Family).*

Many years ago in seminary, I learned this simple definition of what a true disciple is. A *disciple* is *a person who is growing in conformity to Christ, bearing fruit in evangelism, and working in follow-up to conserve his or her fruit.* This beautifully communicates the biblical concept of making a disciple.

During our campus ministry outreach at the University of Auckland in the years 2000-2007, we enjoyed a wonderful surge of students getting saved and developing into vibrant Christian leaders on the campus and in our churches. These leaders were not only dynamic new Christians, but they also had a heart to see their campus changed by the power of Christ. Many of our Christian students became very active and outspoken on the campus, eager to influence their culture for righteousness.

We saw several of the Christian students get involved in student government at the University of Auckland. There were many liberal, secular, anti-Christian clubs operating on the campus at that time, all with a vested interest in who got elected. This was important for many reasons, one being that those elected would determine which campus clubs and organizations would benefit from the distribution of literally tens of thousands of government dollars in university funding.

Our club at the University of Auckland was called Victory Campus Ministry (VCM). Within VCM were several students with strong political aspirations. One such student leader was a bright, popular and talented Tongan girl named Lesieli. She was a natural leader and a passionate Christian. When Lesieli decided to run for the position of student body president at the University of Auckland, we stepped up to support her. It was a position of status and influence for any student to hold, to say the least.

Lesieli crafted a campaign that emphasized integrity and Christian character as her political platform. She was upfront about her Christian convictions and ran a solid campaign. Incredibly, the biggest attack leveled against Lesieli was that she was a *Christian!* It was as if that was the only thing wrong with her they could find. Even worse, it was rumored that she had an agenda that might even be influenced by her Christianity. *Can you imagine that?* Having an elected student official with a Christian agenda?! "Anything, but that!"

What made this story even funnier was the fact that Lesieli was running as an openly Christian candidate. She did not try to hide it. Her faith was never a secret. I will restate a fact that should be painfully obvious to anyone who has ever entered into politics: *the other political candidates have agendas too!* The conservative candidate, the liberal candidate and the green candidate all had agendas!

If elected, the unthinkable might happen: *Lesieli's Christian values might make an impact on the campus.* They might influence her presidency, even the distribution of funds. Now we are getting to the crux of the issue. It was not that each candidate in this race had an agenda, but that Lesieli, if elected, would implement her plans according to a Christian agenda.

The good news is that Lesieli did get elected to the office of president at the University of Auckland. And she did not try to pass legislation that made Bible reading mandatory for students, or make saying Hail Mary's compulsory after attending a biology lecture. Lesieli did, however, serve her term and do an admirable job restoring integrity and trust back to that office. True to her convictions, Lesieli did indeed let her Christian morality and worldview guide her presidency.

With her Christian mindset, Lesieli successfully engaged a confused and spiritually dark campus with the power and truth as an elected leader, centered on Jesus. She was able to sponsor several Christian events and encourage other Christian organizations to unashamedly exercise religious expression and convictions on the campus. The revived openness for Christian groups and freedom to express biblical morals was a refreshing change for students and faculty alike. (And yes, she was able to influence the flow of resources on the campus too.)

The resurgence of a strong Christian voice on the University of Auckland also emboldened many other Christians who were formerly rather timid about their faith to take a stand. It is this kind of intentional engagement that we as Christians must have if we are going to bring God's influence and have an impact in the world.

As believers, we must be in touch with God's agenda. Our personal priorities must line up with His Divine Agenda. Just as Paul instructed the church at Corinth, "Whether then, you eat or drink or whatever you do, do all to the glory of God" (1 Corinthians 10:31). We are to look for opportunities to make the gospel known "and pray . . . that utterance may given to me in the opening of my mouth, to make known with boldness the mystery of the gospel" (Ephesians 6:19).

Why Witness?

It really doesn't matter whether we find engaging with others comfortable or not. There is a compelling need for believers to have the courage and the confidence to talk to others about Christ. As Charles Spurgeon the 19th-century "prince of preachers" once said, "We are not responsible to God for the souls that are saved, but we are responsible for the gospel that is preached and for the way in which we preach it."[12]

As a result, it is important for us to learn how to preach and present Christ well. The reasons are abundantly obvious. We are living in an age of growing skepticism, secular humanism and scientific materialism where the average person is having more difficulty in believing in a God they cannot see.

Unfortunately, many atheists, agnostics and some professing

Christians feel that the church does not have the answers to address these complex issues surrounding modern life. If people choose to ignore or reject Christ after being given a reasonable answer to their questions, that's one thing, but to hear nothing of substance from the Christian community about Jesus' claims as God and Savior is another.

Doubters and skeptics with honest questions have a right to hear a cogent and factual presentation about the veracity of Christianity. Our responsibility is to help them identify, address and work through their legitimate doubts. After that, we are encouraged to let God take care of the results.

What Would Jesus Do?

Back at the turn of the millennium, a trendy Christian cliché circulated around churches and youth groups in America. Christians of all ages started wearing popular jewelry items, T-shirts and hats with the bold letters W.W.J.D. These initials stood for *What Would Jesus Do* and the acronym became very popular and recognizable to both believers and nonbelievers.

While reflecting on one's behavior and comparing it to what Jesus' response might be in a given situation is commendable, unfortunately, many people who don the W.W.J.D. merchandise are not committed to following the advice this question suggests. It's not only about asking *what* Jesus would do, but also about realizing what made Him do the things that He did in the first place. In other words, *why* were Jesus' life and death significant? We should be asking, *Why did Jesus do what Jesus did?*

Jesus' actions and mission were born out of *who He was*. Jesus came to earth as the incarnation of God. He left Heaven and took on the form of man to rescue humanity from sin and death. His earthly actions were a direct correlation to His divine nature and mission. Those who express the desire to follow Jesus now are not just mimicking His actions; they are exuding His very nature through their lives.

Salt without Flavor

In Mark's Gospel an analogy is used to contrast saltiness with tastelessness. "Salt is good; but if the salt becomes unsalty, with what will you make it salty again? Have salt in yourselves, and be at peace with one another" (Mark 9:50). In this passage, *salt* is mentioned in terms of its use as a preservative and also as a seasoning. It is used to emphasize the importance of being a different flavor than the world.

The Scripture warns us that if salt loses its saltiness it is good for nothing except to be thrown out and trampled underfoot. The idea of insipid salt (tasteless, bland and weak) seems to defy and negate the nature and function of salt in the first place. We as Christians are not meant to be like that.

God's initial role for His chosen people, Israel, was to be a purifying agency among the nations of the earth. Matthew records Jesus' address to His disciples: "You are the salt of the earth" (Matthew 5:13). There was a unique flavoring that His disciples were to bring to the world.

Just like the nature and function of salt, the disciples in Jesus' day were intended to have a preserving and purifying effect on those around them. The idea of an insipid Christian ought to be a contradiction in terms.[13]

You are the light of the world. A city set on a hill cannot be hidden; nor does anyone light a lamp and put it under a basket, but on the lampstand, and it gives light to all who are in the house. Let your light shine before men in such a way that they may see your good works, and glorify your Father who is in heaven.

— Matthew 5:14-16

In the above verses, Jesus makes an analogy of a city prominently displayed on a hill, easily seen by all who pass by, and a lamp placed on the lampstand to illumine the whole house. This parable highlights God's plan for us to reflect His glory in our personal lives in such a way that others can see the difference between the Christian life and the status quo of the world.

Part of the problem is that we as Western Christians have compartmentalized religious life. We have our work, our families, our friends, our sports, and somewhere in all of this we try to fit in a little bit of God.

This type of living is antithetical to the call to follow Jesus. The Bible narrative shows us a God who doesn't simply want to be one of our many priorities; He must be *the first* priority. Anything that we insert in His place as a god substitute is nothing short of idolatrous. The Creator of heaven and earth longs to be recognized by all as such.

The Apostle Paul knew that the Lord had specially selected him to share in carrying out the divine agenda. What caused Paul, a zealous Pharisee, to radically change his personal plans, convert to Christianity, and adopt God's agenda? Paul's revelation on the road to Damascus set him apart to serve as an ambassador on Christ's behalf, proclaiming the gospel to the whole world.

Identifying the Divine Agenda

The following five points help us see how God's plan to advance the gospel message is woven throughout Paul's ministry, and indeed the entire New Testament.

1. The Gospel is of First Importance.

> *For I delivered to you as of first importance what I also received, that Christ died for our sins according to the Scriptures, and that He was buried, and that He was raised on the third day according to the Scriptures, and that He appeared to Cephas, then to the twelve.*
>
> - 1 Corinthians 15:3-5

The above is perhaps the most central verse in the entire New Testament, for it contains one of the earliest formations of the Apostles' Creed. Paul recognized God's agenda to spread the gospel news as preeminent. God's agenda became the primary agenda in Paul's life. He gave it *first importance* in his plans.

At this point we might like to ask ourselves, *Do I really give God and His message first importance in my life?* Paul writes to the church in Corinth that he himself established, telling them that they must maintain the same motivation. That was Paul's primary ambition from the get-go: to continue with the preaching of the gospel as the main focus of his ministry, and the ministry of the churches he had planted.

Church history reveals that the Christians at Corinth were an especially colorful and rather dysfunctional group. Corinth was riddled with moral problems that required the Apostle Paul's immediate attention. This was largely due to the fact that during the initial growth of Christianity in the city, Corinth was a port city in the Roman province of Achaia. Corinth was thus a great commercial center that acted as a crossroads to the Middle East, North Africa and Rome - much like Singapore has developed as an international center of trade today. Goods and luxuries from all over the world were transported through the ports of Corinth.

Also located in Corinth was the temple of Aphrodite, the Greek goddess of love. Aphrodite's temple housed over 1,000 cult prostitutes and made the city infamous, to such an extent that during the rule of the Roman Empire the Greek verb *korinthiazomai* became known as a synonym for sexual immorality. Every vice and piece of immoral decadence known to man was available in Corinth.[14]

Paul was very aware of the challenges facing the young church at Corinth. In the midst of this moral decadence, Paul wrote his letter to bring much needed correction. Here are a few of the disturbing issues that Paul addressed in the Corinthian church:

- Reports of division in the church (1 Corinthians 1:10-1:17).
- Scandalous sexual sins of incest (1 Corinthians 5:1-13).
- Threats of lawsuits between church members (1 Corinthians 6:1-11).
- Sexual immorality among Christians (1 Corinthians 6:12-20).
- Church members getting drunk at the communion services (1 Corinthians 11:17-34).

In his letter, Paul also included guidelines for proper Christian behavior:

- Instructions on how singles and married couples should behave (1 Corinthians 7:1-40).
- Guidelines on how Christians were to properly employ spiritual gifts in a public service (1 Corinthians 12:1-40).

The Church at Corinth certainly had some major problems to deal with. No doubt Paul was very concerned over these spiritual deficiencies. They were imposing problems for any church leader to contend with. However, even with all these problems plaguing the Corinthian Church, *Paul insisted that the preaching and the spreading of the gospel must have first importance.*

2. We are Debtors to the Gospel.

The Apostle Paul felt obligated to preach the gospel to the world. In his own words, he was indebted to God to carry out the gospel proclamation to the Greeks, Barbarians and to the Romans. Paul viewed his responsibility to spread the gospel as a debt he owed not only to God, but also to those who had never heard the message.

> *I am debtor both to Greeks and to Barbarians, both to the wise and to unwise. So, as much as is in me, I am ready to preach the gospel to you who are in Rome also. For I am not ashamed of the gospel of Christ: for it is the power of God to salvation for everyone who believes, for the Jew first, and also for the Greek.*
>
> *- Romans 1:14-16 (NKJV)*

Paul uses a word that can be translated as *indebtedness* or *obliga-*

tion. The word *obligated* or *obliged* suggests *a contractual agreement to pay back some favor or loan.*[15] The Apostle Paul thus viewed this new agenda of the spreading of the gospel as a morally binding responsibility. He saw it as a *debt.* Paul understood the preaching of the gospel to be a divine responsibility, an obligation that he was bound to fulfill.

Why did Paul see this ministry of evangelistic engagement as his obligation? Paul, formerly Saul, of Tarsus, had been a very devout Pharisee and a promising Jewish teacher before his conversion experience with Christ. After Paul's encounter with Jesus, however, he was struck blind, only to be healed and have his outlook transformed.

When he was later healed, Paul came to believe that this new sect of Christianity that he had been trying to eradicate was really God's salvation to mankind, as revealed to him by Jesus when He appeared to him on the road to Damascus.

But what does this biblical account teach us? For one, there's no virtue in truth, unless that truth is applied. In other words, with the revelation of *who* God is and *what* He requires, there comes a huge weight of responsibility. Knowledge in some cases brings with it an obligation to take action. That is why some people would rather stay in the dark about it.

The sentiment for some people is to think that it's better to remain ignorant than to get involved in things that may cost them their time, their money or their convenience. It may seem easier for them to turn a blind eye or a deaf ear to others' needs, in an attempt to avoid responsibility.

While living on the North Shore of Auckland, New Zealand, I had to go to the post office one day to buy some stamps and mail a few letters back to the States. The post office was in a beautiful little beach community called Takapuna. Regrettably, I was in a big hurry to get my postal business done and speed off to another appointment, so I didn't linger to enjoy the scenic views.

Being close to Christmas, the line - or "queue" as many British Kiwi would say - to purchase my international stamps was long. Over to my side, I noticed a young mother with three small children looking through the postal supplies. The children were fussy and agitated.

I watched as the mother placed her toddler on a nearby desk while she tended to her other two fussy children. The toddler was in a very unstable situation, and was in danger of falling off the back of the desk onto the concrete floor.

The distracted mother was clearly oblivious to the danger her child was in. I, on the other hand, was aware of a piece of knowledge that demanded my immediate response. I could stay in the line and avoid losing my place, thereby keeping my busy itinerary moving, or I could risk losing my place in line and prevent a potentially bad accident from happening.

Apparently, the other people waiting in the stamp line did not see what was going on with the young mother and her children because no one else moved to help her. Like her, they were completely oblivious to the dangerous situation. But, because I saw the imminent danger, I quickly got out of the postal line and rushed to the toddler, grabbed the teetering child off of the desk and handed her back to her mother. I then mentioned to the lady how potentially dangerous it was for her child to be placed on that table. Flashing an embarrassed smile, the woman thanked me for my help.

This incident stood out to me for several reasons. One, I was extremely busy that day, rushing around trying to take care of all my pressing engagements. Also, if I stepped out to help, I was very aware that I could easily lose my place in line.

I could have attempted another strategy, that would certainly have been much more convenient. I could have called out to her, and hoped that she would turn to save her infant herself - before it was too late, or *I could have prayed that God send some other responsible person to help this mother at that moment.* But I didn't.

Instead, I moved to help the mother and child myself. What stimulated me to action? *I knew something she did not know!* The revelation of that child's real danger made me both nervous and responsible. I was obliged to act, because *knowledge obligates.*

There is a verse in Proverbs that states, "a righteous man has regard [cares] for the life of his beast, but even the compassion of the wicked is cruel" (Proverbs 12:10). In this passage the Hebrew word for *regard* is the word *knows*. It is important to understand that God sees the righteous as having a *caring knowledge* that ensures proper responsibility for the nurturing of those around us - His creation. In contrast, the wicked has no such care for his beast and is to be considered cruel.

According to author and social critic Os Guinness, "Knowledge for the Christian is never noncommittal nor conscience free. Knowledge carries responsibility. Knowing means doing."[16] Unfortunately our culture now exalts the mere acquisition of knowledge without any responsibility to live in accordance with it. Having such a non-committal attitude and approach to life has become very acceptable in our culture.

Nowadays, we can gain much knowledge on an important issue

and still remain passive and detached from the action that ought to go along with it. How many unfit people "know" that being overweight can produce very severe health problems, yet never set foot in a gym or change their eating habits? How many cigarette smokers are informed of the health dangers related to their habit?

Most smokers "know" that their lifestyle is unhealthy and could lead to cardiovascular disease, diabetes, hypertension, cancer and early death. But they do not *know* it enough to change. Possessing this knowledge, they still fail to act on their knowledge, making it of little or no effect. There is no virtue in gaining that information unless it is acted upon.

Yet, *most of us,* if we are honest with ourselves, want information *without* obligation. But that is simply not how life works. Knowledge compels us to act according to the knowledge we have gained. Most Christians know too much to remain silent. Our Bible knowledge has far exceeded our Bible obedience. There is an obligation for Christians to speak out.

3. We have been given the Ministry of Reconciliation.

Therefore, if anyone is in Christ, he is a new creation; old things have passed away; behold, all things have become new. Now all these things are of God, who has reconciled us to Himself through Jesus Christ, and has given us the ministry of reconciliation, that is, that God was in Christ reconciling the world to Himself, not imputing their trespasses to them, and He has committed to us the word of reconciliation. Now then, we are ambassadors for Christ as though

God were pleading through us; we implore you on Christ's behalf, be reconciled to God. For He made Him who knew no sin to be sin for us, that we might become the righteousness of God in Him.

- 2 Corinthians 5:17-21 (NKJV)

Whenever we read the New Testament, it is clear that God's agenda to spread the gospel to the corners of the earth is not limited to a few select ministry superstars, like Peter, Paul or Timothy. God intends for ordinary people, regular Christians, to take this agenda for world evangelization seriously and adopt it as their own.

All believers are meant to be ambassadors for Christ, active ministers who communicate the message of reconciliation to non-believers around them. Again, as our first Rule of Engagement states, we must *accept our mission.* God has commissioned all believers, regardless of status or class, to be His mouthpiece in order to relay what they have experienced to the rest of the world.

4. Proclaim the Gospel with Confidence.

Paul's entire ministry was marked by a reverential and holy fear of God. Paul knew he had been set apart to proclaim the gospel to the whole world (Acts 26:16-18).

"For the king knows about these matters, and I speak to him also with confidence, since I am persuaded that none of these things escape his notice; for this has not been done in a corner. King Agrippa, do you believe the Prophets? I know that you do." And Agrippa

replied to Paul, "In a short time you will persuade me to become a Christian." And Paul said, "I would to God, that whether in a short or long time, not only you, but also all who hear me this day, might become such as I am, except for these chains."

- Acts 26:26-29

Paul needed to walk in confidence to fulfill his assignment to preach to the Gentiles. In order for Paul to attempt, let alone complete his God-given mission, he had to have some assurance that what he was doing would work, that the Jesus he was preaching was who He said He was. Paul needed to know that not only had God commissioned him, but that He was actively helping him with his mission. Just like Paul, contemporary Christians need to sense the *confidence* that comes from an awareness of God's presence when they are ministering to others.

I have a dear friend named John Rohrer. John has a powerful prophetic ministry gift that he uses to encourage people across America, and indeed the entire world. Formerly, he was a college basketball coach before he entered full-time ministry and is affectionately called "Coach" by all who know him.

John preaches a powerful message called "Don't Throw Away Your Confidence, which has a Great Reward." It's taken from the text in Hebrews 10:35. Coach Rohrer understands the great value of having confidence. But what exactly is *confidence*, as Hebrews states it?

Confidence is *the feeling or belief that one can rely on someone or something; firm trust: the state of feeling certain about the truth of something.*[17]

This type of *confidence* is clearly demonstrated throughout the New Testament. In Acts chapter 26, Paul stood trial before King Agrippa II and Festus in order to defend his obedience to believe and preach the gospel. Paul knew full well the kind of man King Agrippa was. By all the natural standards, Paul's life was clearly in jeopardy. He needed divine assurance and divine confidence at that time.

King Agrippa II was the great-grandson of Herod the Great, who decades earlier had attempted to kill the infant Jesus and who ordered the murder of many baby boys in Judea around the time of Jesus' birth. Agrippa II's father, Herod Agrippa I, was also a ruthless ruler and an enemy of Christianity (Acts 12:2). It was Agrippa I who had the Apostle James beheaded and also arrested the Apostle Peter in an attempt to kill him in hopes of silencing the gospel and appeasing the Jews. (Scripture tells us later in Acts chapter 12 that after this encounter with Peter, the Lord became angry with King Agrippa I and struck him dead).

King Agrippa II's family was infamous for its brutality. They ruled the land with an iron fist. They were also quick to eliminate any perceived political insurrection or religious troublemakers. In fact, Paul was fully aware of King Agrippa II's ruthless reputation.

Paul knew full well that he could be facing execution, or at least life imprisonment. But in the midst of this trial, Paul drew upon an inner confidence that transcended his apparently dire circumstances. Paul's personal experiences and confidence are mind-boggling for the average person.

Where did Paul get this confidence? Evidently he had received a big dose of confidence from his *life-altering encounter with Jesus* on the road to Damascus. Before any of this had happened, Paul experienced a divine visitation from Jesus Christ and was struck blind as a result for three days. It was not until a man named Ananias prayed for him that Paul regained his sight. Paul was then baptized and soon became a champion for the cause of Christ (Acts 9:17).

In one moment, the greatest enemy of Christianity became its most ardent supporter. During his early ministry, Paul had seen firsthand evidence of the gospel at work: people were healed, those possessed by demons were delivered, and lives were totally transformed by the gospel (Acts 16:18; 17:10-12; 19:11-12). Paul witnessed the gospel as powerfully effective in converting both Jews and Gentiles to Christianity.

He testified of the power of the gospel to transform the unbeliever to real faith in Jesus Christ, declaring that he was not ashamed of the gospel, and writing to the Church at Rome that *the power of God rests on the proclamation of the gospel*. Paul became not only convinced but also confident of the truth of the gospel's effectiveness in the lives of those who heard and received it (Romans 1:16). He would not stop talking about it, even in prison.[18] Paul's life demonstrated his belief that God had selected and commissioned him as a bearer of the good news, the gospel message (Acts 9:15; 13:2; 26:14-16).

In reality, confidence is essential for any goal or action to be successful. It is not just having confidence in our ability to present a clear gospel message that is enough - although that is important, too. We must be fully convinced that the gospel account of Christ's saving power, love and grace is objectively true. The Christian's confidence is inextricably linked to the real transformative power of the gospel to change a person's life from the inside out.

When we discover what the Apostle Paul experienced centuries ago - *a life altering encounter with Jesus* - we too can have a strong confidence when engaging the world with the power of the gospel.

Let us hold fast the confession of our hope without wavering, for He who promised is faithful.

- Hebrews 10:23

We must be confident that our God will back up our preaching of the gospel with His presence and power. We must be convinced that our message, spoken with the bold confidence that comes from Christ, will be effective. The gospel is God's truth and it is productive because it is God's only way to bring people out of darkness and into eternal life (Romans 1:16). Further, it is our faith that puts sparks to this fire. Like Paul, we can and must proclaim the gospel with great confidence.

5. Knowing the Fear of God, We Persuade Others.

For we must all appear before the judgment seat of Christ, so that each one may be recompensed for his deeds in the body, according to what he has done, whether good or bad. Therefore knowing the fear of the Lord, we persuade men, but we are made manifest to God; and I hope that we are made manifest also in your consciences.

- 2 Corinthians 5:10-11

There is a healthy fear of God that should motivate all believers to be proactive about sharing their faith. The Apostle Paul, when writing his second letter to the church in Corinth, reminded the believers that they would all have to stand before the judgment seat of Christ and give an account for what they had done while alive on earth.

Interestingly, Paul emphasized that their efforts to influence others about the claims of Christ would be a central point of this judgment.

In this context, Paul uses the word *persuade*. To persuade means *to convince or influence others*. It also means *to cause someone to believe something, especially after a sustained effort.*[19]

In other words, Paul exhorted all Christians to actively try to persuade and engage others about the words and message of Jesus' life. Paul understood the reality that all Christians would have to stand before the judgment seat of their Lord. Judgment is imminent. Therefore, what kind of lives ought we to live (1 Peter 1:17; 2 Peter 3:11)? All Christians should have a serious and sober perspective regarding their role in presenting the gospel to others.

Remember, Paul is not writing this letter to vocational pastors and ministers. He is writing it to everyday believers.

A Fragrant Aroma

The Apostle Paul addressed the church in 2 Corinthians 2:15-16, writing, "For we are a fragrance of Christ to God among those who are being saved and among those who are perishing; to the one an aroma from death to death, to the other an aroma from life to life."

Other than illustrating our shared appreciation for sweet smells with the churches of Paul's day, Paul's words are very revealing. This is what they indicate: Not everyone will be drawn to the message of Christ. As Christians we will either exude an aroma that is sweet and attractive to those whose hearts are open to the gospel, or a smell that is putrid and repulsive to those whose hearts are hard and rebellious to the truth of it.

Let's be honest, sharing the gospel is not always a pleasant experience. I have had good experiences, and I have had bad experiences.

Sharing the gospel can be a planned part of my weekly routine, or opportunities can present themselves at unexpected times, and the responses I get really can and do vary from person to person.

On several occasions, I have gone shopping with my wife, Renee, in a department store, when a casual encounter turns out to be just such a type of learning experience. One time while Renee was making a purchase in the cosmetics section, I began sampling the different colognes on display.

Anyone familiar with department stores or the sale of perfume will know that in order to test any given perfume or cologne at the counter, little rectangular cards are provided alongside them. A sample of perfume can be sprayed on one of these so that the particular scent can be inhaled apart from all of the others. I am sure that you have seen what I am talking about. After sampling a few different kinds, it's time to settle on the scent that you like the most. A sales clerk generally shows up about this time to help you purchase it.

But just imagine, for a moment, that someone pulled a prank on me and replaced a bottle of one of these fine and expensive perfumes with a container of stinky sewage water. What would be the response of any unsuspecting customer like myself who happened to inhale it? Instead of encountering a sweet-smelling fragrance, the customer would step back in disgust. Just one single whiff of this foul concoction would be enough to offend almost anyone's olfactory senses. The smell would be rancid and repulsive, certainly not a scent that anyone would ever want to buy. This "perfume prank" would stop almost anyone from pulling out his or her wallet.

According to the Apostle Paul, that is how the gospel smells when a hardhearted person encounters it. It is noxious and repulsive. To some, the gospel is a sweet fragrance. To others, it's revolting. Being nice and winsome is commendable. But our polite behavior will not keep the gospel's aroma of death, from being a stench to the carnal, unrepentant soul.

All this is to say that, in some cases, to choose to avoid controversy for fear of giving offense is to choose to avoid Christ. As Russell Moore astutely observes:

> Too many attempts at reconciling Christianity and the outside culture have to do with being seen as relevant by the culture on its own terms. We will never be able to do that. Culture is a rolling stone, and it waits for no band of Christians seeking to imitate it or exegete it.[20]

Today more than ever, it is imperative that people know what the Bible says and what the gospel message is. It is important that people know how to share what God has done for them through the free sacrifice of His only begotten Son, Jesus Christ. Pastors, churches, missionaries and leaders of parachurch ministries must educate and disciple their people in the context of historical, orthodox Christianity - and do so in accordance with its content. The equipping of all believers for the work of ministry is part and parcel of the church's responsibility to the world it was appointed to reach (Ephesians 4:12-13).

The nature of the gospel message makes it a stumbling block to some people. But that does not diminish the believer's responsibility to clearly present the gospel. Instead of trying to soften it to appeal to people, Christians need to accurately preach and teach the gospel, appealing to its power as the only force strong enough to change the heart of man.

All Things to All People

To the weak I became weak, that I might win the weak; I have become all things to all men, so that I may by all means save some. I do all things for the sake of the gospel, so that I may become a fellow partaker of it.

- 1 Corinthians 9:22-23

This sharing of the gospel must be done with flexibility and consideration. It is clear from Paul's exhortation to the church at Corinth that he wanted to keep the goal of reaching the lost world paramount in his life and ministry.

The concept that Paul is writing about here is often called *contextualization* by theologians and missiologists. *Contextualization* means simply *translating the gospel in both words and actions that can be adequately understood by a particular target audience.*[21] In other words, whenever we present the gospel it should be in a manner and in a language that those who hear it can understand. You want your listeners to comprehend the message you are sharing.

The verse in 1 Corinthians 9:22 in no way suggests that a Christian needs to compromise his or her Christian morals in hopes of appeasing a non-Christian pagan Corinthian, or in order to win credit with them. The truth of the gospel speaks for itself.

In fact, becoming "all things to all people" does not mean fitting into the fallen patterns of this world's system. It does not mean conforming to the point that there is no distinguishable difference between the Christian and the non-Christian. So don't let your evangelism strategy render the gospel unclear or confusing to the people you are trying to reach. Share God's truth from Scripture, and let the gospel speak for itself.

Paul's primary objective was to make the good news available by any means possible. That must remain our primary concern as well.

Some skeptics have posed the question, *"What about those who have never heard of Jesus? Will they go to hell when they die?"* Assuming Christianity to be the truth, if I am truly concerned about the unreached people groups in the world, the best thing for me to do is to get saved and go out and reach them.

C. S. Lewis wrote in *Mere Christianity,* "If you are worried about people outside of Christianity, the most unreasonable thing you can do is remain outside of it yourself."[22] This statement exposes the hypocrisy of those who criticize Christianity without making the commitment Christianity requires.

Accept Your Mission

"Go and make disciples of all nations" (Matthew 28:19). By this we know at least two aspects of God's divine agenda: 1) preach the gospel to the world and 2) make disciples in every nation. Jesus commissioned all of His followers to be agents of His Eternal Kingdom.

We also know that the extent of God's agenda is not limited geographically or culturally. "This gospel of the kingdom shall be preached in the whole world as a testimony to all the nations, and the end will come" (Matthew 24:14).

Christians armed with God's agenda and mission will be characterized by an eternal perspective on life and will engage the world with a compassion for the lost and a passion to spread the truth of Jesus.

CHAPTER THREE

The Gospel Message

True gospel preaching always changes the heart . . . It either awakens it or hardens it.

- Chan Kilgore[23]

Since the birth of Christ until the present day, the most effective means of spreading the Christian faith has been through personal communication. That is why it is essential that we ensure our gospel presentation is clear and easy to grasp.

This is the way the angels announced the birth of Jesus to the shepherds (Luke 2:8-20) and the way the Magi announced the birth of Jesus to Herod (Matthew 2:1-12). Personal evangelism is effective because it is truest to the heart and to the experience, the easiest to deliver and to organize.

There are a lot of opinions concerning *how* to go about sharing one's faith with non-Christians. Many believers have tried to copy the results of other Christians by duplicating a particular evangelism tool or technique. When well-meaning individuals try to duplicate a process without embodying the personal revelation and passion that formed it, not only is the message weakened, but the effect can be that they strengthen people's resistance to the truth of the gospel as well.

Evangelistic methods, techniques and tools are important, but they can never replace the power of the personal conviction and zeal gained as a result of having applied the truth of the gospel message to one's own life. Our fruitfulness is more dependent upon our conviction concerning the truth and our life of intimacy and obedience with the Lord, than upon the techniques we use. The Christian message expressed through the lives of individual believers is powerful because it is personally owned and acted upon. It is also powerful because it is true. Such passion can express itself in a hundred different ways.

Historically, some of the greatest testaments to the effectiveness of the Christian witness were actually made by opponents of the faith. A second century philosopher named Celsus was a fierce opponent of Christianity. Celsus wrote how Christians possessing little or no education seized every opportunity to witness to people, and when confronted by educated pagans they still would not stop presenting the gospel message. Personal evangelism in this context was quite powerful because it was often backed up by outstanding acts of kindness. For example, during outbreaks of the plague in Alexandria, Christians tended the sick and buried the dead when nearly everyone else had fled. The lifestyle of these Christians was among the most powerful contributor to the effectiveness of Christian evangelism.[24]

Ask fifty self-professing evangelical Christians what the gospel message is, and you are likely to get almost as many answers. Likewise, if you listen to evangelical preaching or log on to various evangelical websites, you will find many varied and even conflicting descriptions of the gospel. In fact, there are many available tools that have been developed to communicate the gospel, often emphasizing different aspects of the salvation message.

Some popular methods would include the *Four Spiritual Laws* (now known as "The Four") laid out by Cru. Cru is an interdenominational Christian parachurch organization for college and university students formerly known as Campus Crusade for Christ. Another tool is the *Bridge to Life* used by the Navigators, and the *Steps to Peace with God* used by the Billy Graham Crusades. Good approaches to sharing the gospel will place emphasis directly on the Scriptures relating to salvation, as shown for example in the "Roman Road" approach to sharing the gospel using the Book of Romans.

Many people mistake meeting new people through events or serving people's needs in compassion ministry as evangelism. Although serving the lost, the poor, the widow and the weak is part of showing the compassion of Christ to those made in His image, meeting physical needs without meeting their spiritual need to hear the gospel, is not evangelism.

Evangelism is sharing the gospel, so that those who hear the message can receive the power to get saved. The gospel, once heard, received and acted upon will transform a person, empowering them to rise up out of their poverty, addictions, and pain. If we only offer people temporary earthly comforts, without offering them the opportunity to receive spiritual transformation in Christ, we will continually rob them of their human dignity by encouraging their codependency upon others.

Jesus recognized this when He declared: "The Spirit of the Lord is upon Me, because He anointed Me to preach the gospel to the poor" (Luke 4:18a). John the Baptist also understood the importance of preaching the Gospel to the poor (Luke 7:22), recognizing this would be clear evidence that Jesus was the Anointed One.

Many churches host a variety of events that serve their community in many ways. Hopefully these events are being utilized as access points for the guests to be invited into deeper connection where they will be personally presented the gospel. Whatever settings, events or outreach approaches you use, be aware of the needs and culture of the people you are reaching out to, and do your best to be on the same page with your team helping organize the event.

➢ Rule #2: Clarify Your Message.

So, what exactly *is* the gospel? Paul, in the Book of Acts, highlights the importance of the gospel message: "When he had seen the vision, immediately we sought to go into Macedonia, concluding that God had called us to preach the gospel to them" (Acts 16:10). The Greek word in this verse is *euangelizo*, which *means proclaim glad tidings*. The gospel is literally the *good news*. From this word *euangelizo*, we get the English word *evangelize*.[25]

There is, however, a danger of presenting a gospel message that is inauthentic. The Apostle Paul warned the church in Galatia not to receive a *different gospel*. "I am amazed that you are so quickly deserting Him who called you by the grace of Christ, for a different gospel" (Galatians 1:6). Obviously, Paul felt called to confront a counterfeit and false gospel masquerading as the truth.

Over the years, I have heard many abbreviated, man-centered and even faulty gospel presentations used and abused. The authentic gospel message has necessary components, which if left out, can cause an individual to have a truncated or incomplete understanding of what the good news really is.

A biblically sound gospel presentation is essential and brings understanding for salvation. The gospel must be presented in both the fear of the Lord and the love of God. As such, it must include a *recognition of God's divine nature* as perfectly holy and just in contrast to the fallen, sinful state of humanity. It must impart an understanding of the merciful sacrifice and necessary substitution of Christ as the payment for mankind's sin.

The gospel when fully preached carries within it the power to transform a life. Paul states:

"For I am not ashamed of the gospel of Christ, for it is the power of God to salvation for everyone who believes, for the Jew first and also the Greek. For in it the righteousness of God is revealed from faith to faith; as it is written," The just shall live by faith"

- Romans 1:16-17 (NKJV)

The gospel, when preached should provoke *a response of conviction, sorrow, and repentance* resulting in the forgiveness of sins, followed by *a willingness to surrender to Jesus Christ as Lord and Savior.* If the message is received, the result will be a beautiful new creation. And this is only the beginning. New believers will commit themselves to becoming disciples and witnesses of Christ.

If the gospel we are preaching does not include these basic elements, then it is not a gospel that can save. Therefore, it is imperative that we accurately preach, teach and present the complete gospel message to others.

Here's another way to think about it. Have you ever seen anyone on television or at a sporting event hold up a sign that states, *Jesus is the answer?* As Christians, we do know that Jesus is the ultimate answer. He is indeed the solution. The only problem is that most people don't even understand *what* the problem is. Before the *answer* is able to make any sense at all, we must first identify and understand the nature of the *problem.*

Sometimes the answer may not be enough. A person does not take the trouble to go to a doctor unless he or she is sick. What if I said to you in a conversation, much like the ending of the 2005 movie, *The Hitchhiker's Guide to the Galaxy,* "The answer is 74"?[26] Even if I repeated the correct answer over and over, "The answer is 74. The answer is 74. The answer is 74," etc. the answer would make no sense to you until I finally stated the problem which the answer would solve.

If, instead, I had asked you the question, "What does 55 + 19 equal?" Then, "The answer is 74," would make perfectly good sense. It would be understood in the context of the math problem. Just as knowing the solution to this math problem made no sense without first seeing the math problem, the correct answer, Jesus, will make no sense to those who have never understood the problem of mankind's sin. As carriers of the gospel message, we must first properly frame the problem of humanity's sin and resulting separation from God. Only then will the groundwork be laid for the solution that God offered for humanity's sin: Jesus Christ.

As ministers of reconciliation, we need to be able to bring individuals into an understanding of the state they are in, *lost and separated from the life of God, because of their sins.* Jesus was not just a good moral teacher or a misguided martyr. We must be able to present the answer of Christ crucified in a proper setting, so that people may be able to grasp the truth, God permitting, of why the gospel is indeed the good news.

Seven Key Words

If you're strapped for time or memory space, you can simply use what I like to call "the 7 S's" to remember that the gospel can be expressed in just seven key words. Using and understanding these words can sum up the theological significance of the gospel, in a simple, straightforward explanation of why Jesus is indeed the only answer. Here are the 7 S's.

1. SIN
2. SEPARATION
3. SACRIFICE
4. SUBSTITUTION
5. SORROW
6. SURRENDER
7. SALVATION

1. SIN

In the beginning God, who is perfect, holy and just, created man and woman to walk in an upright and loving relationship with Him, their Creator.

Unfortunately, Adam and Eve chose to disobey God, thereby plunging all humanity into sin. Through their disobedience, sin entered the world. The following Scriptures express this change, known in theological terms as the fall of mankind.

For all have sinned and fall short of the glory of God.

- Romans 3:23

For all of us have become like one who is unclean, and all our righteous deeds are like a filthy garment; and all of us wither like a leaf, and our iniquities, like the wind, take us away.

- Isaiah 64:6

2. SEPARATION

Man's disobedience brought about a spiritual *separation* between God and humanity. The willful sin committed by Adam and Eve stained and contaminated all of humanity. The result of this sin was a great separation, rather like a chasm or gulf, between a holy and righteous God and sinful mankind.

Immediately after they sinned, Adam and Eve tried to hide their sin and shame by sewing fig leaves together to cover their nakedness. But there was nothing they could do to remove their guilt.

For the wages of sin is death . . .

- Romans 6:23

Behold, the LORD's hand is not so short that it cannot save; nor is His ear so dull that it cannot hear. But your iniquities have made a separation between you and your God, and your sins have hidden His face from you so that He does not hear.

- Isaiah 59:1-2

Adam and Eve, like so many of us today, attempted to hide their sin by running from God and covering their nakedness with fig leaves. However, their attempt was insufficient. The justness of God required that the price of sin be paid, for the relationship to be restored.

3. SACRIFICE

A *sacrifice* always points to the giving of something of great value in order to redeem someone or something.[27] In the context of the Garden of Eden, immediately after Adam and Eve sinned, God stepped in to kill an innocent animal and provide a covering for them. "The Lord God made garments of skin for Adam and his wife, and clothed them" (Genesis 3:21).

To pay the penalty for humanity's rebellion against a holy and perfect God, there had to be an innocent sacrifice. The provision of this sacrifice was necessary to appease God's wrath.

The first sacrifice following the fall of mankind in the Garden of Eden occurred through the bloodshed of an innocent animal to clothe Adam and Eve. God providing a covering for Adam and Eve through the shedding of blood, an act which was a foreshadow of what Jesus would one day do for all humanity. Jesus was to become the perfect, sacrificial "Lamb of God."

> *The next day he saw Jesus coming to him and said, "Behold, the Lamb of God who takes away the sin of the world."*
>
> - John 1:29

4. SUBSTITUTION

Without Jesus freely giving His life for all humanity, there would be no atonement for our sins and no emancipation from our fallen, sinful nature. He became, in effect, the *substitution* for us in our sins. Merriam Webster's Collegiate Dictionary defines *substitution* as *one that is substituted for another.*[28] In practical terms for you and me, this means that even though we rightly deserve death and judgment, Jesus substituted Himself for us as a living, perfect sacrifice.

Though Jesus did not deserve death, He chose to suffer and die on the cross in our place, appeasing God's righteous wrath against sinful, fallen humanity. By shedding His blood, Jesus purchased for all mankind the forgiveness of sins, providing the only way for mankind to be reconciled back into relationship with God.

The idea of forgiveness is a powerful concept when it is viewed in the light of God's perfect holiness and human fallenness. Paul writes of the amazing forgiveness extended to humanity by Christ, "In Him we have redemption through His blood, the forgiveness of our trespasses, according to the riches of His grace which He lavished on us" (Ephesians 1:7-8). The word "forgive" is from the Greek word *aphiemi*, which means *to permanently dismiss, to liberate completely, to discharge, to send away, or to release.*[29]

When Paul uses this word *aphiemi* to describe the forgiveness of sins, he is saying that because of the blood of Jesus, God has "permanently discharged" and "totally dismissed" our sins from us, and that all of our past transgressions have been canceled out and forgotten by God. "As far as the east is from the west, so far has He removed our transgressions from us" (Psalm 103:12).

Often, when speaking to university students about God, I find it necessary to emphasize this point about the magnitude of God's forgiveness. I usually ask them if they have ever borrowed money in the form of a student loan to pay for their tuition. In most cases the answer is yes. I then inquire about the amount of their debt. Many of the students will acknowledge that they owe tens of thousands of dollars in school loans. I have actually talked to students who owe over a hundred thousand dollars in student loans toward their undergraduate degree alone! I then pose a few questions like, "What if I came up and gave you a check for the whole amount of your student loans? In an instant your debt would be paid in full. What would you feel about your life and about me as a person?"

They say things like, "I'd be overjoyed. I'd be so thankful to you for your kindness. I would have a party and you'd be the guest of honor. I'd feel so relieved about my future thanks to your gift." I then tell them that is exactly what Jesus did with the debt of their sins. They can cash the check through faith, godly sorrow, repentance and full surrender and be released from their sin debt to God.

This arrangement is good news any way you look at it! "He made Him who knew no sin to be sin on our behalf, so that we might become the righteousness of God in Him" (2 Corinthians 5:21).

5. SORROW

At the beginning of the New Testament we find John the Baptist preparing the way for human hearts to receive the coming Jewish Messiah by preaching a message of repentance to the people.

"Repent, for the kingdom of heaven is at hand!" For this is he who was spoken of by the prophet Isaiah, saying: "The voice of one crying in the wilderness: Prepare the way of the LORD; Make His paths straight."'

- Matthew 3:2-3 (NKJV)

John is telling the people to change their ways, to turn away from practicing sin, and to believe in the coming Messiah. Some clarification is needed here. True repentance is not just about changed behavior. People can change their behavior for many selfish reasons. Some people choose not to indulge in sinful behavior simply because they are afraid of what other people might think of them. This means that their good behavior, which could include regular church attendance, is not necessarily evidence that they have surrendered their lives to Christ. True repentance is based upon godly sorrow.

Godly sorrow is not the same thing as regret or just feeling remorseful or guilty about something. For example, many people feel very sorry for the messes they have gotten themselves into through a series of bad decisions. This sorrow is worldly and does not produce godly results. It may even be a form of self-pity. Feeling conviction over having sinned is not necessarily evidence of true repentance, either. Deep feelings of conviction that are *not* accompanied by true godly sorrow and changed behavior will actually fortify a *false sense of security* or spiritual pride, resulting in callousness, deception and religiosity.

A fear of going to hell and being punished, can motivate some people to change their ways temporarily, but fear is also self-centered and does not produce lasting change. A god-centered sorrow is the precursor to lasting change.

A godly sorrow over sin, is born out of grief that we have sinned against a holy God and broken *His* heart. This sorrow will result in true repentance. This repentance is not something that can be earned; it is a *gift* from God (2 Timothy 2:25). It cannot be gained through manipulation and tears (Hebrews 12:17). This godly brokenness over sin will produce in a person a decision to turn away from anything that the Bible calls sin and would offend a Holy God. This godly sorrow over the ownership and cost of personal sin will change the way a person views sin for the rest of their life. It will pierce their heart (Acts 2:36-38).

Godly sorrow results in an *action* called repentance. The following Scripture expresses this understanding of *repentance* well:

> *For the sorrow that is according to the will of God produces a repentance without regret, leading to salvation, but the sorrow of the world produces death. For behold what earnestness this very thing, this godly sorrow has produced in you; what vindication of yourselves, what indignation, what fear, what longing, what zeal, what avenging of wrong! In everything you demonstrated yourselves to be innocent in the matter.*
>
> - 2 Corinthians 7:10-11

True repentance cannot be separated from godly sorrow. True repentance is initiated by godly sorrow and results in turning away from everything the Bible calls sin. True repentance involves a change of heart, a change of mind and a change of direction. Repentance is a gift from God and true repentance will be without regret.

Another important aspect of repentance is that it is required to receive forgiveness of sins. "John the Baptist appeared in the wilderness preaching a message of repentance for the forgiveness of sins" (Mark 1:4). It would be incomplete to tell someone that Jesus will forgive them of their sins without also telling them that Jesus requires that they repent and walk in obedience to His Lordship.

In the story of the prodigal son in Luke 15:11-32, for example, we see a story of repentance and forgiveness in the actions of a father and his younger of two sons. The younger son asks his father for his share of the inheritance before his father's death.

Apparently he had no desire for relationship with his father or older brother. He cared less about their feelings and their future than about spending the money his father had promised him in his will. All he really cared about was getting what he wanted, when he wanted it. And he wanted his share of the inheritance, *now*!

Does this sound like anyone you know? After squandering all of his wealth, and his so-called friends abandoned him, this young man found himself working on a pig farm on the verge of starvation. *A pig farm, of all places!* As a Jewish man, this would have been about as humiliating as it could get. But worse than that, he was so hungry that he even wanted to eat the pigs' food!

Scripture says that at that point, "he came to his senses" realizing what he had done and how he had behaved so selfishly sinning against his father. He then decided to go home and make things right with his dad, hoping that he would be merciful and at least take him on as a servant. When he reached home, however, to his amazement his father, who had been looking for him, ran to him, embraced him, and reinstated him as his son that very day.

Not only is this a compelling tale of the power of forgiveness and the love that our Heavenly Father has for us, but it is a beautiful story of the humble, penitent and grateful heart that our Heavenly Father longs for us to display. Repentance, motivated out of a godly sorrow, will result in restored relationship with the Father.

When presenting the gospel, it is important not to rush things, but to allow the Holy Spirit time to work in the person's heart this godly sorrow that leads to a true repentance. Jesus Himself exhorted His disciples "that repentance for the forgiveness of sins would be proclaimed in His name to all the nations" (Luke 24:47). It must have been important to Him.

6. SURRENDER

After Jesus' resurrection, on the day of Pentecost, Peter took his stand and preached: "Therefore let all the house of Israel know for certain that God has made Him both Lord and Christ, this Jesus whom you have crucified" (Acts 2:36). Peter proclaimed God's sovereignty as His choice of Jesus as both Lord and Christ, the Messiah. He reminded the people that their sins had put Jesus on the cross.

The people were pierced to their hearts and cried out, asking what they should do. Peter responded by commanding the listeners to, "Repent, and each of you be baptized in the name of Jesus Christ for the forgiveness of your sins; and you will receive the gift of the Holy Spirit" (Acts 2:38).

In other words, the people were called not only to repent and believe, but, to *surrender. Surrender* is *an act in which resistance to a perceived opponent or enemy stops forever. It is an act of submission to demonstrated authority.*[30]

Full surrender and submission to Jesus Christ as Lord are the entrance point into the Kingdom of Heaven. It is followed by repentance from dead works, the obedience of baptism, and receiving the Holy Spirit. This is the evidence of adoption as His son or daughter.

> *But what does it say? "The word is near you, in your mouth and in your heart" that is, the word of faith which we are preaching, that if you confess with your mouth Jesus as Lord, and believe in your heart that God raised Him from the dead, you will be saved.*

> - Romans 10:8-9

7. SALVATION

Salvation comes from the Greek word *soteria*, which means *to bring deliverance and preservation from danger.* The root word is *sozo*, and that means *wholeness and soundness of health*, thereby giving *salvation* a medical connotation.[31] In biblical terms, however, salvation is deliverance from the bondage of sin and its eternal consequences. Salvation is brought about by trusting alone in Christ's atoning death, burial, and resurrection. Moreover, salvation is the assurance that those who believe are redeemed by grace through faith in the finished work of Jesus Christ.

> *And there is salvation in no one else; for there is no other name under heaven that has been given among men by which we must be saved.*

> - Acts 4:12

For with the heart a person believes, resulting in righteousness, and with the mouth he confesses, resulting in salvation.

- Romans 10:10

Luke tells the story of Zacchaeus, a tax collector from the city of Jericho. As Jesus was preaching in that city, Zacchaeus, who happened to be small in stature, climbed up into a sycamore tree to see and hear Him teach. To the dismay of the other Jews, Jesus accepted the invitation to stay at Zacchaeus' home. As evidence of a changed heart Zacchaeus announced to his house guests, "Behold, Lord, half of my possessions I will give to the poor, and if I have defrauded anyone of anything, I will give back four times as much" (Luke 19:8). Zacchaeus showed the depth of his repentance by his desire to restore his relationship to others.

What was Jesus' response when He saw the results of a contrite and repentant tax collector? "And Jesus said to him, 'Today salvation has come to this house'" (Luke 19:9). Here we see Jesus stating his primary purpose in coming to earth: "For the Son of Man has come to seek and save that which was lost" (Luke 19:10).

The Good News

Telling people simply that "Jesus is the answer" or that "God loves them" will not get the job done in the skeptical, relativistic culture of today. Believers must be able to present the gospel message articulately and coherently to a non-Christian world. For non-believers to understand, Christians must be equipped to present the gospel with a precision and passion that will cause scales to fall from the eyes of non-believers.

If you are still feeling uncertain about how to present the good news, here are a few other well-known, theologically sound statements of the gospel presentation.

1. The gospel is the glorious proclamation of God's redemptive activity in Christ Jesus on behalf of man enslaved to sin.[32]

2. Through the person and work of Jesus Christ, God fully accomplishes salvation for us, rescuing us from judgment for sin into fellowship with Him, and then restores the creation in which we can enjoy our new life together with Him forever.[33]

3. The gospel is the good news that God became man in Jesus Christ. He lived the life we should have lived, and died the death we should have died, in our place. Three days later, He rose from the dead, proving that He is the Son of God, and offering the gift of salvation and forgiveness of sins to anyone who repents and believes the gospel.[34]

4. The gospel is the good news that the just and gracious Creator of the universe has looked upon hopelessly sinful men and women and has sent his Son, Jesus Christ, God in the flesh, to bear His wrath against sin on the cross and to show His power over sin in the resurrection, so that ev-

eryone who turns from their sin and themselves and trusts in Jesus as Savior and Lord will be reconciled to God forever.[35]

The future of Christianity cannot be assumed just because we have some big churches and Bible teaching aired on cable T.V. on Sunday mornings. While we do know that Christ and His Kingdom will be pronounced victorious in the end (Philippians 2:10), it cannot be assumed that the Christian social witness will be accepted and retain its roots in the culture from now till then.

As Os Guinness points out:

> Our age presents the greatest opportunity for the Christian witness since the time of Jesus and the apostles, our response should be to seize the opportunity with bold and imaginative enterprise. If ever the 'wide and effective door' that St. Paul wrote of has been reopened for the gospel, it is now.[36]

Made Righteous by Grace

It must be emphasized that receiving the gospel message or having a conversion experience is not the result of human works or effort. There is nothing we can do that can merit God's redemption. We are not "entitled" to salvation. We are not "victims" that need to be "rescued." We are sinners, enemies of God that need to take responsibility for our lives by repenting for our sins and gratefully serving Him for the rest of our lives, because of who He is: Creator, Savior, and Lord (Romans 5:10; Philippians 3:18).

But God, being rich in mercy, because of His great love with which He loved us, even when we were dead in our transgressions, made us alive together with Christ (by grace you have been saved), and raised us up with Him, and seated us with Him in the heavenly places in Christ Jesus, so that in the ages to come He might show the surpassing riches of His grace in kindness toward us in Christ Jesus. For by grace you have been saved through faith; and that not of yourselves, it is the gift of God; not as a result of works, so that no one may boast. For we are His workmanship, created in Christ Jesus for good works, which God prepared beforehand so that we would walk in them.

- Ephesians 2:4-10

It is Finished

On the cross, Jesus breathed His last breath with the words, "It is finished" (John 19:30). There is nothing that we can add to the completed work of Jesus Christ through His death, burial and resurrection. "But God demonstrates His own love toward us, in that while we were yet sinners, Christ died for us" (Romans 5:8). Jesus accomplished the work that He was sent to do. He gave His life in exchange for ours. His sinless death on the cross forever removed the penalty for our sin. We cannot earn salvation through our own good works. We can only be saved through the power of the gift of God's grace alone. Even the best gospel presentation, without the grace of God, is not able to save.

When the grace of God apprehends a person's heart, there is a moment where the miracle of the "new birth" or "salvation" takes place. "Jesus answered and said to him, 'Truly, truly, I say to you, unless one is born again he cannot see the kingdom of God'" (John 3:3). God warned Adam in the garden that if he disobeyed Him and ate from the tree of the knowledge of good and evil, that he would die (Genesis 2:17). "Therefore, just as through one man sin entered into the world, and death through sin, and so death spread to all men" (Romans 5:12). This death was both spiritual and physical. Jesus is speaking of a second, spiritual birth when He told Nicodemus that he must be born again: made a new creation (2 Corinthians 5:17), made alive with Christ (Ephesians 2:5).

Other contemporary terms which are meant to express the salvation experience include "getting saved," "turning your life over to Jesus," or "committing one's life to Christ." Theologically these terms are synonymous for becoming a Christian.

Jesus purchased back many privileges for us through His sacrificial death on the cross. "The wages of sin is death, but the free gift of God is eternal life in Christ Jesus our Lord" (Romans 6:3). Through Christ, God achieved what we could not: Christ perfectly fulfilled every requirement of the law so that now, "we are free to live, not according to our flesh, but by the dynamic power of the Holy Spirit!" (Romans 8:4 TPT).

The following divine benefits are available to the believer by way of the amazing grace of God.

Righteousness:	**2 Corinthians 5:21**
Justification:	**Romans 3:24**
Redemption:	**Psalm 19:14**
Forgiveness:	**Acts 10:43**

| Reconciliation: | Colossians 1:19-20 |
| Sanctification: | Hebrews 10:10 |

Not only have we been forgiven and reconciled back to God, Christ now resides richly in us enabling us to walk by the Spirit, putting to death the deeds of the flesh (Galatians 5:16). "This gospel unveils a continual revelation of God's righteousness - a perfect righteousness given to us when we believe. And it moves us from *receiving life through faith*, to *the power of living by* faith" (Romans 1:17 TPT). Peter goes on to describe our new identity and purpose in Christ:

> *But you are a chosen people, a royal priesthood, a holy nation, God's special possession, that you may declare the praises of him who called you out of darkness into his wonderful light.*
>
> - 1 Peter 2:9 (NIV)

A Prayer for Salvation

As mentioned before, we cannot save ourselves by our good deeds or by trying harder to follow God's commands. We stand guilty and condemned against the perfect holiness of God's standard. It is only by the mercy and grace of God that any of us can be redeemed through the sacrifice of Jesus (Ephesians 2:8-10). It is only by placing our faith completely in what Jesus Christ has done for us, and not in what we have done, that we can receive the gift of salvation.

"It is by grace that you are saved, through faith" (Ephesians 2:8).

James 4:6 continues, "God is opposed to the proud, but gives grace to the humble." The Holy Spirit will never forcefully make anyone follow God's plan for salvation against their will. We must be willing to approach God in humility. Humility is the key to receiving the gift of salvation.

"But as many as received Him, to them He gave the right to become children of God, even to those who believe in His name, who were born, not of blood nor of the will of the flesh nor of the will of man, but of God" (John 1:12-13).

Seven key elements to include in a prayer of salvation:

1. **Express true sorrow for your sins (2 Corinthians 7:10).**
2. **Repent (turn away) from all known sin (Acts 3:19).**
3. **Ask God to forgive your sins (1 John 1:9).**
4. **Stop trusting in your own efforts or religious good works to be good enough (Titus 3:5).**
5. **Put your faith and trust totally in what Jesus Christ accomplished on the cross (Ephesians 2:8-9).**
6. **Receive Jesus Christ into your heart as your Lord and Savior (Romans 10:9).**
7. **Commit to obeying God's word, the Bible, and to growing in your new relationship with God (1 Peter 2:2).**

Here is a sample prayer for salvation that you can use in order to lead someone to Christ. I would recommend that you lead them through the entire prayer having them say these words aloud, pausing after each phrase so they can verbally repeat the phrase after you. In fact, if you have never repented for your sins and asked Jesus Christ to come into your life as Lord, trusting in Christ alone for your salvation, this would be a great time to pray this prayer:

> *Lord Jesus, I am sorry for my sins . . . I turn from everything that You and the Bible call sin . . . I ask for You to forgive me . . . I choose to stop trusting in myself and what I can do . . . and to start trusting in what You have already done when You died for me on the cross, were buried and rose again from the dead . . . I surrender to You as my Lord and Savior . . . I ask You to come and live inside me and cause me to be born again . . . I totally commit myself to obeying You and Your Word every day for the rest of my life . . . Thank You for dying for me on the cross . . . Thank You for hearing my prayer and accepting me as Your son/daughter . . . Jesus, You are my Lord and Savior and I will serve You the rest of my life. In Jesus' name, Amen.*

CHAPTER FOUR

Christic in You

God became man to turn creatures into sons: not simply to produce better men of the old kind but to produce a new kind of man. It is not like teaching a horse to jump better and better but like turning a horse into a winged creature.
- C. S. Lewis[37]

As writer and Oxford-educated scholar C. S. Lewis affirms, the gospel of Jesus Christ is transformative. It doesn't just improve us: It makes us into whole, new beings. It radically changes our nature and the entirety of our perspectives on life. We become something we were not, but were very much meant to be.

In Need of Change

Someone once said that variety is the spice of life. I think it's just the other way around. *We* add variety to life because *we* are bored, empty, unsatisfied, and without purpose. Many people try to break the monotony and staleness of their everyday lives by getting new things like a new car, a new job or taking vacations to new exotic places. Sadly, this year's Christmas gifts will probably serve as fodder for next year's garage sales.

There are those who make New Year resolutions to lose weight and exercise more in hopes that self-improvement will satisfy their deep longings and make their lives better. For these people, the end of the year is often met with broken self-promises and the disappointing return of bad habits. We can waste years of our lives trying to satisfy this inner emptiness with trivial pursuits and addictions, before recognizing that we are incapable of changing ourselves.

Mankind, on his own initiative will never admit his need to be reconciled with God and be transformed. Paul, quoting Isaiah, states that "There is none who seeks for God; all have turned aside, together they have become useless; there is none who does good" (Romans 3:11-12). If we are honest with ourselves, we will eventually admit that the transformation we need to take place in our lives cannot be rendered by us, no matter how hard we try. We are desperate for God to intervene.

God's plan from the beginning was to put His Spirit in us and make us new creations. If your faith has not transformed you, it probably has not saved you. *There should be evidence of Christ's presence in you.*

A Rendezvous with Destiny

There comes a time in a person's life when God's purpose and destiny become so clear that they can no longer be denied. That moment happened for me back in graduate school. God interrupted my life. I could no longer run away from God's plans or ignore His clear calling upon my life.

It was during this time that my football buddy invited me to come to a Christian meeting being held on the campus at Tennessee Technological University. A young evangelist named Rice Broocks was the guest speaker. Rice was advertised as a "football star" that had played at the University of North Texas. As a former football player myself, I was intrigued. I came along to the meeting to hear what this former athlete had to say about Christ. As Rice preached, I found myself under such great conviction about my sin that I could not ignore it. I knew that what he was saying about Jesus was true.

That night, on August 1st, 1980 in Cookeville, Tennessee, everything changed. I was confronted with the bold proclamation of the gospel. I had an encounter with God that radically changed me. I prayed then and there and asked Jesus to forgive me and to take control of my life. I knew without any doubt that God had mercifully saved me and called me to live for Him. Not only did I get "saved" but God made a shift in my heart that redirected the course of my entire life. I had dreamed of being a college football coach and teaching at the university level, but, strangely enough, God gave me an inner peace and confidence to take a radical step of faith. I knew God had called me into full-time ministry. It was inescapable. I had been changed from the inside out.

Real Change

I will never forget the time that Renee and I went to Honolulu to see my eldest daughter, Rebecca, who attended the University of Hawaii and played on the Rainbow Wahine basketball team there. We were also scheduled to minister at Grace Bible Church in Pearl City. I was walking around our hotel when I started a conversation with a young man sitting by the pool. We chatted for a few minutes, learning about each other, and then he asked me where I lived. I told him that I lived in New Zealand (we were missionaries there at the time) and that my wife and I, and other children were in Hawaii visiting my daughter at the university.

He blurted out, *"Wow, New Zealand!* What an awesome place!" The man proceeded to talk about how "cool" it would be to visit and live in New Zealand. He went on to say that he would do *anything to* get a chance to go and visit New Zealand.

I asked him, "How do you like living in Honolulu?"

Without a second's hesitation, he said, "It's very depressing, man! I don't like it at all." He went on to tell me how bad things were in Hawaii and how he needed a change of location to improve his life and really get ahead.

I thought to myself, "We are standing in front of Waikiki Beach, surrounded by the gorgeous Pacific Ocean, drenched with sunshine, shaded by palm trees, with a gentle, tropical breeze blowing into our faces, and *you are depressed?* Are you kidding me?" We were in absolute paradise, and this guy wanted *a change of scenery* so he could be happy.

I was gob-smacked by his perceived dilemma. I told him that if he was depressed in Honolulu, he would certainly be depressed in New Zealand too. It wouldn't matter how exotic and beautiful it was.

Puzzled, he stared at me, and then asked, "What do you mean?" I responded, "The trouble is, you'll have to bring yourself along with you wherever you go. Wherever you end up, *you'll* be there too." I went on to explain, "If you're sad and unhappy in Honolulu, it's just a matter of time before you'll be sad and unhappy in New Zealand as well. Your problem is an internal problem not an external one." I then had the opportunity to tell this young man about how to find true satisfaction and contentment in knowing and following Jesus.

No matter where you live, there are problems you will face. This universal recognition that things in this world are not as they should be, not the way we deeply want them to be, is inherent to every human soul. I am convinced that what people are truly yearning for is an inner transformation. While new cars and exotic holiday locations may bring temporary changes, only spiritual transformation can bring about lasting change.

You Must Be Born Again

People's problems do not arise from their current car, job, or location, but they arise from their *internal condition*. It is the condition of a person's heart and soul that makes them sad or happy. There is no guarantee that a change in geographic location will help anyone for very long, or help anyone at all ultimately. As Jesus said to Nicodemus, "You must be *born again*" (John 3:7 emphasis mine).

Spiritually speaking, there must be an internal change. The Bible refers to this internal change as being "made new," or given a "new nature," or make you a "new creation." If you are not born again, Jesus tells Nicodemus, "You cannot *see* the Kingdom of God" (John 3:3 emphasis mine). This means that you will never be able to perceive or comprehend things from God's point of view.

As Christians, our greatest attribute, our most attractive feature, is that we have been changed and made into new creations in Christ. It is the message of His love and forgiveness that empowers us and gives us life.

It is Christ *in* and *active in* us that is the real hope of glory.

The Effect of the Gospel: Transformation

And do not be conformed to this world, but be transformed by the renewing of your mind, so that you may prove what the will of God is, that which is good and acceptable and perfect.

- Romans 12:2

I remember as a child watching in complete amazement a furry little caterpillar spin its cocoon and then emerge a few weeks later, a totally different creature. What was once a worm crawling around among the leaves was now a beautiful winged butterfly, soaring freely in the sky. An incredible transformation had taken place.

Transformation is about *an internal, lasting change* that is obvious to others. The word that the Apostle Paul used to communicate this amazing change is the Greek word, *metamorphoo,* which literally means *to change, to transfigure, transform.*[38] We derive our English word *metamorphosis* from that same Greek word. Just as creeping caterpillars change into beautiful butterflies, God can change the nature of people too.

A Changed Perspective

I will never forget an encounter I had in Auckland, New Zealand with a man over a cup of coffee one Friday afternoon. He was a Samoan gentleman by the name of Poutoa, who was a successful businessman running for the office of city council. Poutoa was not the type of man you encountered lightly.

His daughter, Nadeen, attended my church and had informed me that her father was running for election for a political post. I had asked Nadeen to arrange an appointment with her dad.

When we met, Poutoa and I exchanged some pleasantries as we sat down in a little café to order our coffees. Poutoa knew I was a minister and fully expected me to talk to him about spiritual matters. Instead, I began by asking him about his political life and his family and the love he had for them. Poutoa also spoke of how he wanted to provide governmental legislation that would help Polynesian families prosper across New Zealand. I asked Poutoa why he was affiliated with a political party that was anti-family and hostile to the values that he believed in and cherished.[39]

He looked at me with a puzzled expression, and replied, "This is the party that will help me get elected to office. That's why." I pointed out that there was a severe conflict of interests between his personal family values and his political party affiliation. I then encouraged him to think about running as an independent candidate. Poutoa said that, given the current political climate in Auckland, it was almost impossible for him to get elected as an independent candidate. We finished our coffees and ended the conversation.

He started attending our church and soon committed his life to Jesus. His family and his friends began to see other differences in Poutoa. Not only did he change as a person, but his political aspirations too began to change. A few weeks later Poutoa called me and said, "Ken, I have decided to run for office as an independent candidate."

Poutoa ran in the election as an independent candidate and was elected to the councilman seat in Auckland. Poutoa is now an active church member, a devoted Christian husband and father, and a born-again civic leader representing his community.

One consistent feature that marks Christianity as a movement is its ability to affect change and bring about influence, not only at the personal level, but also in the culture that surrounds it. Christ in you is not just about receiving personal forgiveness so that you can have your ticket punched for heaven. It is about allowing God's destiny and purpose to be expressed through your life. The moment we are changed by God's power, we embark upon a lifelong adventure to let Him use us to advance His kingdom to others.

➢ Rule #3: Live Your Message.

As Dallas Willard once wrote, "The gospel affects everything, starting with the heart of a person, then radiating out into our homes, to our friends and our businesses, touching every fabric of our lives."[40] And that's the way it should be.

The gospel message is life-giving and it should affect every aspect of our existence. As such, it ought not to be pushed aside. Too many times people allow the academic elites, the scientific community, or the popular consensus to decide what counts as reality, while religion is consigned to the outskirts of public life as a matter of personal opinion or private belief. There could hardly be a decision more damaging to society or more misguided in its approach to truth than this.

We see in the Gospels of Matthew, Mark, Luke and John that where Jesus went and ministered, dramatic changes took place. No one who encountered Jesus was ever left the same.

The Gospel of John records the account of Jesus' first miracle at the wedding in Cana of Galilee (John 2:1-12). When the wine ran out, Jesus' mother informed Him that there was no more wine at the event. Jesus replied to His mother that His time had not yet come, however, at the insistence of His mother, Jesus instructed the servants to fill six stone water pots with water. Upon receiving Jesus' instruction, the servants then drew some of the water (now transformed by Jesus into wine) and took it to the headwaiter for a taste test. When the headwaiter tasted the wine, he was amazed at its quality. The headwaiter then announced, to his surprise, that this wine was the finest wine of the day, knowing that traditionally, the best wine was served when the guests first arrived. This was the first of many miracles Jesus was to enact.

There are a couple of conclusions that we can draw from this incident. We see that Jesus cares about people, about weddings and celebrations. He is considerate of the needs of others, and He was obedient to His earthly mother, Mary. But most importantly, it is clear from this story that Jesus did not just desire to be a blessing to people. Here we see ordinary water transformed into wine. Even the nature of water could not stay the same at His command. But Jesus didn't just come to change water into wine. He came to transform lives.

Later on throughout the course of His healing ministry, Jesus saw the lame walk, the blind see, the deaf hear and the mute speak. Anyone who Jesus came into contact with was changed for the better. When we come to God and freely give Him our life, He will in turn transform it.

The following is an amazing story of how one student's life was changed forever.

Bart's Transformation

"On May 13, 1986 one of my teammates invited me to a presentation at the Georgia Tech Student Center being sponsored by a campus ministry group and being led by Ken Dew. The Holy Spirit used this presentation entitled, 'Rock 'n' Roll: A Search for God,' to open my eyes to the reality of Jesus Christ and to the spirit world.

"As Ken preached at the end of the seminar, I understood for the first time in my life that Jesus Christ is real and that He died on the cross for my sins. I realized that I was lost and if I died that I would go to hell apart from Jesus. However, because of fear, I didn't respond to the altar call at that moment.

"My teammates and I left quickly after the presentation was over, but thank God, Ken, being sensitive to the Holy Spirit, left the altar call and pursued us outside the theater into the student center lobby. He began to speak with us about our thoughts on the presentation and asked us if we were Christians. Another teammate and I agreed to have lunch with Ken.

"The next day, Ken shared with me his story over lunch at the Georgia Tech Athletic Center. Also, he told me that as he was praying for me that morning, the Lord showed him that two people were specifically praying for me. I instantly knew that was the truth, as my mother and sister definitely were praying consistently for me.

"I told Ken that I had tried to change my lifestyle at different times because I felt guilty, but I never could do it for long. Ken then shared and explained to me from John chapter three what it really means to be 'born again' and receive the Spirit of Jesus into my life. At that point, he asked me, 'Are you ready to surrender your life to Jesus?' I told him yes, so we went upstairs to a study hall room in the athletic center.

"Ken led me in a prayer of repentance and faith, and I knew something had happened in my life. Later, as I went to class I sensed the presence of God in my life for the first time. Moreover, after my class, I went back to my dorm room and began to read a few Scriptures from my Bible that Ken had written down for me. For the first time, the Lord spoke to my mind and heart directly by His Spirit through the Scripture, and I was amazed!

"As a result of this amazing 24-hour period of time in my

life, I got involved in a campus ministry group at Georgia Tech and began to get discipled in the teachings and truths of Jesus. Upon graduation, I worked in corporate America for almost two years and was actively involved in campus ministry in Atlanta. The Lord began to speak to me to leave the marketplace and to join Him in the work of reaching and teaching students for Christ on university campuses.

"For the last twenty-eight years I have been a Christian minister evangelizing and working with university students teaching them about Jesus."[41]

Bart Jones currently serves as the Ministry Director of *Forerunners for Christ,* an evangelistic ministry located in Atlanta, Georgia. Just like Bart's life was transformed when he humbled himself and surrendered to Christ, any person can fundamentally be changed when they encounter the Lord.

Peter, who denied Christ three times (John 18:15-27), was later transformed by the Holy Spirit and Jesus Christ's resurrection power. He was transformed to such an extent that, on the day of Pentecost, Peter took his stand and "raised his voice and declared to them . . . Therefore, let all the house of Israel know for certain that God has made Him both Lord and Christ, this Jesus whom you crucified" (Acts 2:14, 36).

Peter was so utterly transformed by the outpouring of the Holy Spirit upon his life that he became the leader of this new sect of Christ's followers, called Christians, and literally "turned the world upside down" (Acts 17:6 AMP).

During our first year in New Zealand we started holding Saturday night "Home Group" meetings. Renee and I moved our family into a large home that occupied seven acres of land on the North Shore of Auckland. It was here on Saturday nights that the church of Every Nation Auckland was birthed. Not only did the unsaved come to our home groups, but also many believers came that had never experienced God's healing power.

One particular night in February 2000, a young, newly engaged Christian couple named David Coss and Kim Burrows, attended a Bible study hosted in our home. Having been invited by a friend, they were curious to check out this group of American Christians who had just moved to New Zealand.

I remember there were about fifteen people sitting in our lounge as I conducted the Bible study. At the end of the study I asked, "Is there anyone who needs prayer for physical healing?" Kim raised her hand and explained that she had severe back problems. Kim showed us her pillow, a lumbar compression cushion, that she carried with her and would use in order to try and alleviate her back pain. Kim was only twenty-two and had suffered with constant severe back pain since she was nineteen years old.

Kim also had to wear a compression bandage on her knee at all times and was unable to walk up a single flight of stairs. If there were no elevator, she would have to crawl up the stairs. At times her knees and back would give out, and she would collapse to the ground in agony. Kim's biggest fear, now engaged, was that she wouldn't be able to walk down the aisle on her wedding day. She related how Satan had constantly lied to her that she'd never be able to be a normal wife or a mother.

That night everything changed for Kim when she encountered God's miraculous transforming power. We sat Kim in a wooden chair and extended her legs to compare their length. One leg was easily two inches shorter than the other. Renee and I then anointed her with oil and prayed that God would do a miracle. In the presence of our Bible study group, the shorter leg instantly grew out to be the same length as the other leg. We then prayed for her chronic back pain and knee problems.

Within minutes, Kim was walking and jumping around the room without pain. She was totally healed that night from all of her issues, and she and David got married. Kim did walk down the aisle, and they now have five beautiful children.

As a result of being physically healed by God, Kim and David dedicated their lives to following Jesus Christ. Twelve years later, David and Kim were instrumental in helping to establish our Every Nation Church in Brisbane, Australia. In 2016, they also relocated their family for four months to help with a new Every Nation church plant on the Islands of Fiji. After all these years Kim's back is still healed and strong, and her changed life is a tribute to God's transforming power.

Apprehended by the Gospel

Saul of Tarsus, a self-avowed enemy of Christ, was on the road to Damascus to arrest and imprison followers of Jesus. Saul had been trained with the equivalent of two PhDs as a lifelong Pharisee and understudy to the famous Jewish rabbi and leader of the Sanhedrin, Gamaliel. On the way to Damascus, however, he was miraculously changed by a visitation from the Lord (Acts 9:1-19). Saul came to understand that Jesus was the true Messiah prophesied by the Jewish Scriptures.

It is interesting to note that Jesus appeared to Saul *without warning or permission*. Jesus had an agenda!

"Saul, Saul, why are you persecuting Me?" And he said, "Who are You, Lord?" And He said, "I am Jesus whom you are persecuting, but get up and enter the city, and it will be told you what you must do."

- Acts 9:4-6

The encounter blinded Saul for three days and left him soul-searching. However, he obeyed the message Jesus gave him and after a period of three days without eating or drinking, the Lord prompted a man named Ananias to come and pray for him to receive sight. When Ananias came and prayed for Saul, Scripture says that scales fell from his eyes, and he was filled with the Holy Spirit.

Saul was converted to Christianity, and God forgave him of his religious pride and self-righteous attitude. God revealed to Saul His plan for his life, that he would be called to suffer for the sake of Christ's name. Saul of Tarsus, formerly a devoted follower of Judaism, now had a new purpose and direction and became the man we now know as the Apostle Paul. His encounter with Christ not only affected him, but it had an amazing effect upon the development of Christianity, Scripture, world history, and culture.

Saul was seeking and hunting the believers in Damascus who belonged to the Way to persecute and arrest them. He wanted to bring them to Jerusalem to stand trial (Acts 9:1-2). What Saul found on his way, however, was an encounter with a Person that would change and reconfigure the direction that his life was going. As a result of this encounter, Saul dedicated his life to proclaiming Jesus as the *Messiah* to the rest of the world, Jew and Gentile.

This encounter with Jesus changed Saul's whole world, and showed him that truth was more than the result of study or a line of thought. Truth was a *Person* and truth was *The Way.* Saul was fully convinced that Jesus was *The Truth* and Christianity was *The Way.* As a result, his name, his identity, and the course of his life were radically changed.

The frequent expression, "to walk in the ways of God" or "the Lord" is derived from the Greek word *poreuomai,* which means *to pursue the journey on which one has entered, to continue on one's journey, to order one's life.* In fact, in Jeremiah 5:4, obeying God's law is referred to as *"the way of the Lord."* [42] The *Way* is universally understood with reference to God's leading in the individual's life.

After Paul's conversion, he became devoted to the propagation of the Christian message of redemption by grace. Paul's new life in Christ and the story of how he got there were a vital part of the message that he preached. The point of these Scriptures for us now is that God's truth implied a particular *Way.* It was true because God said it, and it was also true because it worked and was meant to work in the lives of those who believe and follow Him. Christianity was originally known as *The Way* because of its practical applications and the way that it affects daily human life and people's interaction with one another.

Since all of God's redemptive plans point toward humanity's salvation, God's path to salvation is referred to as "His Way." Consequently, His divine plans center on Christ. He is *The Way* to God the Father (John 14:6).

A Heart Transplant

Let's take a look at Jesus' encounter with the Pharisee, Nicodemus (John 3:2-3). Here we find Nicodemus, who by all accounts was a devout Jewish ruler, eager to learn more from Jesus about the phenomenon called becoming "Born Again."

Nicodemus approached Jesus, affirming Him as a teacher and acknowledging that Jesus' miracles proved Him to be a messenger sent from God. Jesus immediately offered Nicodemus a diagnosis and a cure for his spiritual condition: "You must be born again." This statement confounded Nicodemus and he asked, "How can a man be born when he is old?" This is a physical impossibility. Instead of attempting to explain biology, Jesus answered by saying, "Unless one is born again he cannot see the kingdom of God." Jesus perceived that Nicodemus was looking for more than just another outward religious activity to help him find temporary inner peace. And He knew exactly how to respond: "Do not be amazed that I say to you, you must be born again."

Why is this statement, this response Jesus gives, so significant? It is important because it shows that the real change Jesus is looking for, has to be internal, a transformation of the heart. Heart-transformation must occur on the inside before lasting change can occur on the outside. One must be born again before one can really, truly live.

In 2 Corinthians 5:17, Paul writes, "Therefore if anyone is in Christ, he is a new creature; the old things passed away; behold new things have come." Paul is emphasizing a total transformation for those who are in Christ. This amazing regenerating grace creates a new world in the soul and a new way of living altogether.

This new creation is very different from the former. The renewed man acts from new principles, has new aspirations, lives by new rules, with new ends, and in new company. Paul concludes (verse 18) by reminding us that the agent of change is God Himself. He then explains

God's motivation in offering us change: "Now all these things are from God, who reconciled us to Himself through Christ and gave us the ministry of reconciliation."

God transforms us so that we, as new creatures in Christ, can be restored into relationship with Him and can affect change in others. This is a vivid picture of how Paul engaged his culture with the gospel of Jesus Christ as an agent of change. Paul truly believed that he carried the essence of the Truth that could transform others, just like it radically transformed him. Paul also believed that repenting from sin and receiving the transformation that Christ offered was the first step in this transformation process. He went on to train, teach and disciple his young converts to become *complete* and *mature* in the things of Christ

It is important to be culturally sensitive, but it is more important for Christians to realize that the catalyst that brings about change is not our own winsomeness or polite manners, but the power of God.

As Paul wrote to the believers in Colossae, the transformation that people experience when they encounter the risen Christ is the hope of His glory not just for themselves, but also for those around them. Paul instructed the believers to proclaim Him (Colossians 1:28), not just believe in Him and be quiet. *To proclaim* here does not mean to speak only if everyone is agreeable. It literally means *to speak emphatically* about Him, about Jesus and His transforming power, the power that brings about change in men and women's hearts.[43]

Earlier in his writings to the Christians in Rome, the Apostle Paul wrote that he was "not ashamed of the gospel, for it is the power of God for salvation to everyone who believes, to the Jew first and also to the Greek" (Romans 1:16). Paul not only believed the gospel was effective in changing the hearts of his Jewish countrymen; he also believed it had a universal application. *It is understood in Scripture that the gospel is not just the proclamation of the truth, but also, the demonstration of a changed life produced by that truth.*

The Apostle Paul was convinced that the gospel message contained the power of God to convict and to transform the human heart. Furthermore, he was convinced that the word of God has astounding ability to metamorphose the lives of those individuals who accept its authority and that this strengthened its claim as Special Revelation from God.

As Norman Geisler writes:

> The transforming power of the Scriptures has always been one of the strongest evidences of its own divine origin. Untold thousands of individuals down through the centuries have been converted and societal reforms have resulted from the application of the biblical teachings.[44]

I am convinced that we should present the Truth as Christ presented it and Paul proclaimed it. Without a clear presentation of the gospel message, a seeker-sensitive approach to ministry will not bring about transformation in the individual.

Agents of Change

Today many seeker-sensitive ministries have tried to soften or eliminate any offensive elements of Christianity. Instead of seeing the power of the gospel transform lives and culture, we are seeing the culture transform the gospel, attempting to morph it into something more like a

98

spiritual self-improvement program, rather than the powerful, life-giving message of Christ's eternal life and love offered to us by His own gracious hands. The gospel is more than just "one of many ways" to find peace and self-fulfillment. It is *The Way*.

If Christians continue to absorb secular culture instead of being agents of change, there will be no discernible difference between Christians and non-Christians. Without any tangible differences between believers and unbelievers, the world will have no real examples that will inspire them to desire Christ.

As writer, social critic and theologian Os Guinness puts it,

> at the very heart of the dynamic surrounding Christian conversion is the realization that death comes before life, law before grace, and conviction of sin before regeneration. As a result, the "good news" becomes the best news ever to those who know they are in a bad situation.[45]

Remember, every person must first recognize that they are "lost" before they can be "saved." If anything else in the world can satisfy a person's soul, that person is probably not ready for God's solution.

The Christian life is not static, but a lifelong process of becoming more like Jesus and adopting His desires and will as our own. In other words, we as Christians are an integral part of God's plan to redeem and restore the world. And we are certainly not of the world's system. Because we have been transformed by the power of Jesus living in us, we have become *countercultural:* called to citizenship in the Kingdom of God and called to live as strangers on earth.

The gospel brings transformation to those who will receive it as God's truth. The real evidence of the gospel's power is in its ongoing ability to change millions of individual lives. That is why Satan comes to steal the Word. It is the truth sown into the human heart that can change it (Mark 4:14-15). Believers at all times are intended to be righteous agents overcoming the world with transformed lives and hearts full of God's truth.

Right now the Christian church has an unprecedented opportunity to be where the action is. Today, people are hungry for a spiritual community and something certain to believe in. They are looking for an alternative to the hopelessness produced by our self-indulgent lifestyles and chaotic, consumer-driven culture. They are looking for real change. Selfishness makes us keep our faith strictly personal, afraid to integrate it into the rest of our lives or even talk about it for fear of being judged harshly.

Ultimately Christians are to live a life that reflects the changes that Jesus has made in them to become a person whose thoughts, desires and actions have been transformed by the power of Christ's blood. Down through the centuries, transformed men and women have always been the distinguishing mark of historical, biblical Christianity. Those believers, through the grace of God, were enabled to overcome a fear of being rejected by the world, and instead, impact their world by being salt and light to their generation.

For the Glory of God

Paul tells us that *everything* we do should be for God's glory. "Whether, then, you eat or drink or whatever you do, do all to the glory of God" (1 Corinthian 10:31). God is greatly interested in everything that we do: what we say, what we watch, what we listen to, and how we conduct ourselves.

But why is this often so difficult? The problem is that mankind in general wants to share in God's glory. There are biblical examples of this as well. We see in Scripture that King Herod Agrippa II was struck down because he did not give glory to God:

The people kept crying out, "The voice of a god and not of a man!"
And immediately an angel of the Lord struck him because he did not
give God the glory, and he was eaten by worms and died.

- Acts 12:22-23

King Agrippa did not die because he was wealthy and successful, powerful or great. He died because he took for himself the praise and glory that were meant for God alone. Clearly, then, there are consequences for not giving glory to God, whether one is a Christian or not. But Paul wants to remind us as Christians, that the goal of our serving in evangelism and bringing people to salvation is not for our own glory, but it is to bring glory to God.

So that at the name of Jesus every knee will bow, of those who are
in heaven and on earth and under the earth, and that every tongue
will confess that Jesus Christ is Lord, to the glory of God the Father.

- Philippians 2:10-11

The Christian life is dedicated to our Lord and Savior, Jesus Christ, by whose transforming power manifest through us, we can contribute to the glory of the One, True God.

Strong in Grace

Grace is the capacity to do anything spiritually profitable.
You can't pray without grace. You can't understand the Bible
without grace. You can't choose right from wrong without
grace.

- James MacDonald[46]

We know that it is by grace that we have been saved
(Ephesians 2:8-9). Grace is also involved in the sanctification process.
Paul urged the new believers "to continue in the grace of God" (Acts
13:43). When writing of the sanctifying grace of God, Paul told the Co-
lossian believers, "As you received Christ Jesus the Lord, so walk in Him"
(Colossians 2:6). Well, when I received the Lord, I was helpless, broken
and dependent upon His grace.

That is why Jesus said, "My grace is sufficient for you"
(2 Corinthians 12:9). That means that we are to continue to walk each
day in total dependence upon His grace. Timothy also exhorts us to, "Be
strong in the grace that is in Christ Jesus" (2 Timothy 2:1).

Perhaps you have heard someone casually say, "Oh well, grace,
grace. God will forgive me." These people do not have a correct understanding of the purpose of the grace of God in believers' lives. Grace is
not a license to sin.

For certain persons have crept in unnoticed, those who were long be-
forehand marked out for this condemnation, ungodly persons who
turn the grace of our God into licentiousness and deny our only Mas-
ter and Lord, Jesus Christ.

- Jude 1:4

102

It is the grace of God that actually empowers us to walk in freedom from sin. James tells us: "'God is opposed to the proud, but gives grace to the humble.' Submit therefore to God. Resist the devil and he will flee from you" (James 4:6-7).

It is important when engaging the culture that we learn how to lean heavily upon God's grace. This is what Paul had to say about his own integrity and conduct:

> *For our proud confidence is this: the testimony of our conscience, that in holiness and godly sincerity, not in fleshly wisdom but in the grace of God, we have conducted ourselves in the world, and especially toward you.*
>
> - 2 Corinthians 1:12

When Opposition Comes

There have been several occasions that I have been invited to speak at a pre-game chapel service for a sports team. Most of the time, coaches and players see the chapel service as a spiritual pep rally of sorts, a way to fire up their team and help them get a win. Of course, the gospel is much more than that.

There was one particular university where I was asked to speak to the football team prior to a big rival game. To my surprise, an individual approached me beforehand and suggested that I should *not* use the name of Jesus in my talk or during my prayer.

I was a bit surprised by his request. This guy informed me that he felt it would be better for me to refer to Jesus as "God" in the universal or generic sense. That way, the agnostic, Buddhist or Muslim players would not feel excluded or get offended. I listened as politely as I could to the advice of this well-meaning guy. I then told him that I was sorry because I could not comply with his request.

I said, "I would really like to help you, but the coach has asked me to speak to the team, and he is well-aware of the content of my message." I then went on to deliver the chapel service, with frequent mention of the name above every name, *Jesus*. I don't believe anyone got offended, but they did win the game. This experience did confirm one thing to me. *Jesus and what He stands for can be controversial and even threatening to some.*

Today, many non-Christians consider historic Christian beliefs and practices to be offensive and intolerant. According to David Kinnaman:

> Surveys show that two out of five adults believe it is *extreme* to try and convert someone to their faith. This means that evangelism, one of the central acts of Christianity, if not *the most central*, is viewed as "controversial" and "extreme" by 83 percent of atheists and agnostics in America, to say nothing of the views held by the so-called Christian population.[47]

For practical purposes, what this means is that when we engage the culture around us with the gospel message, there is likely to be some resistance and even intolerance. A casual reading of the four Gospels will reveal that Jesus' life and message created a storm of controversy (John 7:12, 41). That is actually one reason why He attracted so many followers!

In fact, at its conception Christianity looked a little like a troublemaker's religion. It wasn't exactly the fastest way to win friends or influence people. In the beginning Christianity was often associated in the public consciousness with conflict, riots and imprisonment (Acts 8:1-3). The historic record also serves as notice that both the political and religious orders of his day considered Jesus and His followers to be dangerous extremists *if* their views were taken seriously and applied to the political and cultural climate of their day (although Jesus made it quite clear in John 18:36 that His Kingdom was *not* of this world).

Of course, it was not generally the Christians who carried out the riots. But throughout the growth of the early church in Jerusalem, Antioch, Macedonia, Rome and elsewhere, thousands of Christians were imprisoned, tortured and killed for Jesus' name. We must look history squarely in the face as Christians and realize that *even its founder was executed as a common criminal* (Luke 23:33).

The Roman writer Tacitus records that after Christ's execution:

> A most mischievous superstition, thus checked for the
> moment, again broke out not only in Judea, the first source
> of evil, but even in Rome, where all things hideous and
> shameful from every part of the world find their center and
> become popular.[48]

Since the earliest days, then, Christians have been redeemed but also stigmatized by this radical message of grace, truth and love. It only stands to reason that we will at times be perceived as radicals and extremists, as well. This is just as Jesus and His followers were treated. We have this promise:

> *Blessed are you when men hate you, and ostracize you, and insult*
> *you, and scorn your name as evil, for the sake of the Son of*

Man. Be glad in that day and leap for joy, for behold, your reward
is great in heaven. For in the same way their fathers used to treat
the prophets.

- Luke 6:22-23 (emphasis mine)

We can expect similar resistance to what Jesus faced when we
try to introduce skeptics or atheists to Christ. Jesus told us that there
would be some people who would follow and obey our message, while
other people would persecute and hate us as they did in Jesus' day
(John 15:20). Nevertheless, we are to love and pray for those who persecute us (Matthew 5:44).

In fact, persecution is no excuse for us to stop sharing the gospel. Paul said he was very familiar with insults, distress, difficulties and
persecution (2 Corinthian 12:10). We must keep in the forefront of our
thinking that Jesus is *the only* message of eternal truth and power, and that
we have been entrusted with it. "He is the way, the truth, and the life"
(John 14:6).

What must be remembered, however, is that atheists, agnostics
or skeptics are not our real enemy. This is the case even as Christians
are persecuted and killed around the world. Those who oppose the gospel are often not even in touch with the origin of their own hostility
toward God. Just because they are sinners does not mean that they are
aware of their condition. Sinners have been blinded by the real enemy
(2 Corinthians 4:4).

Our struggle is essentially in the spiritual realm, not in the physical. The reality is that this battle is not to be fought with physical strength
or with military weapons. It is first and foremost a spiritual battle for the
souls and hearts of men and women around the world.

Fallen humanity is held captive by the enemy's ideas, bound by false, demonic philosophies. The kind of engagement we are talking about in *Engaging the Culture* is intended to help set people free from their captivity by this enemy. Christians, armed with the gospel message of Jesus Christ, strategically deployed and empowered by the Holy Spirit are to be mighty instruments for evangelizing the world.

David Kinnaman has expressed this well:

> In our present culture, many sincere Christians are feeling overwhelmed, sidelined, judged and misunderstood. The sense for many believers is that society is hostile to faith in general and to Christianity in particular. These feelings aren't just imagined. When we see one-third of college-aged adults want nothing to do with religion, and 59 percent of Christian young adults dropping out of church in their twenties, we realize the battle is really on.[49]

Scripture also affirms: "If you were of the world, the world would love its own; but because you are not of the world, but I chose you out of the world, because of this the world hates you" (John 15:19). And, "You adulteresses, do you not know that friendship with the world is hostility toward God? Therefore whoever wishes to be a friend of the world makes himself an enemy of God" (James 4:4).

After reading the above verses, you might think that Jesus is contradicting Himself. But He isn't. God is not double-minded about His people or their mission on the earth. Jesus knows full well that His followers will be in hostile territory while living in this world. He encourages His followers to transcend this world's system, acknowledging their job as Christians is to infiltrate the world, so to speak, and to influence it for the sake of God's Kingdom. The central portion of the Lord's Prayer is about this mission.[50]

There are no nations, institutions or people that are gospel-proof. There is no part of the world that can flourish and survive exempt from God's redemptive presence. The name of Jesus has all authority; "at the name of Jesus every knee should bow, of those in heaven, and of those on earth, and of those under the earth" (Philippians 2:10). It is God's desire for "all men to be saved and come to the knowledge of the truth" (1 Timothy 2:4). What this means for you and me as Christians is that we are to influence culture, rather than let culture influence us.

The reason Christianity has spread around the globe is that our Christian faith presupposes that the whole world needs to know and confess Jesus Christ as Lord. Every person on the earth has the right to hear the gospel and to choose heaven, thus escaping hell. Many martyrs died in Rome to denounce Jupiter as god. Countless missionaries died in a thousand pagan religious systems just to testify there is no saving faith that does not begin and end with Jesus.[51]

Therefore, it is of infinite importance that the Christian church does not miss this opportunity. Believers must step up and engage their worlds with this divine right to hear and to receive the gospel message along with its eternal benefits. The key power of the Bible's message is the *conviction* that it is in fact true. It is not merely a social construct or a psychological crutch to help people cope with hardships in life. Bible truth is universally and objectively true for people in every culture and in every country, in every time and place. Jesus' beloved disciple, John, reminds us: "And you will know the truth, and the truth will set you free" (John 8:32).

If we believe the gospel to be God's only instrument of saving mankind from eternal judgment and the pain of separation from a good and gracious God's love, we must take what C. S. Lewis wrote to heart: "Christianity is a statement which, if false, is of no importance, and, if true, is of infinite importance. The one thing it cannot be is moderately important."[52]

Nancy Pearcey comments:

> Christians are called to tear down mental fortresses and liberate people from the power of false ideas. This process is sometimes called pre-evangelism because its purpose is to prepare people to hear and understand the gospel message. Once the walls are torn down then the message of salvation is the same for everyone, scientist or artist, educated or uneducated, urban or rural.[53]

Every person on earth should be given the chance to receive the message of God's kindness and grace, have the opportunity to go to heaven and escape eternal punishment and isolation from God. Peter wrote, "The Lord is not slow about His promise, as one counts slowness, but is patient toward you, not wishing for any to perish but for all to come to repentance" (2 Peter 3:9).

The great Dutch reformer Abraham Kuyper also said, "There is not a square inch in the whole domain of human existence over which Christ, who is sovereign over all does not cry out: 'Mine!'"[54]

If anything is clear from the Christian witness throughout the ages, it is that God's eternal plan of redemption remains strong. And, in practical terms, it is totally predicated on believers delivering His message and circulating it throughout the whole world.

In the end, then, God's desire is that every person now living hears the truth about Him and the eternal life He offers. Jesus said, "This gospel of the kingdom shall be preached in the whole world as a testimony to all the nations, and then the end will come" (Matthew 24:14).

CHAPTER FIVE

Overcoming Fear

To be fearless in the Lord does not require us to be great and powerful men, but only to believe in the great and powerful God.

- R. J. Rushdoony[55]

Fear is a very powerful emotion. The fear of man or, more precisely, the fear of what other men or women might think about us, is a very powerful fear indeed. I once heard a preacher say, "If you really knew *how little* people actually thought about you, you wouldn't worry so much about *what* they thought about you." The truth of that statement can bruise our ego just a little bit. Nonetheless, the fear of man is one weapon that the enemy has successfully used to silence many Christian voices from speaking out in public.

Let's face it. We all want to be liked by our friends and peers. We want to be invited to the right parties, and rub shoulders with the right people. Virtually everyone grows up craving recognition, popularity and respect. Our reputation is something that we cherish and want to preserve at all costs. There is nothing wrong with wanting other people to think well of you. After all, "A good name is more desirable than great riches; to be esteemed is better than silver or gold" (Proverbs 22:1 NIV).

Remember the phrase, "What will the neighbors think?" All the worrying about what the neighbors thought caused a generation of people to hide their behavior behind closed doors, afraid to get honest with themselves, with others, or with God. Sometimes it just doesn't matter what the neighbors think. What does matter at the end of the day is: *What does God think?* There are people that are literally paralyzed into inaction because they are afraid of what someone else *might* say about them.

The writer of Proverbs uses a very vivid illustration to define the fear of man. The word says, "The fear of man brings a snare, but he who trusts in the Lord will be exalted" (Proverbs 29:25). The word *snare* is very interesting here in this verse, because when we speak of a snare, we usually think of a small trap with some bait laid in it to attract and capture an unsuspecting animal. This picture depicts *a hunter* and *the hunted*. We have probably all seen animal snares on popular nature shows like National Geographic or Animal Planet. The animal steps into the trap, the snare is sprung, capturing the animal by a leg or its neck.

The word that is translated as *snare* in Proverbs 29 is similar. It is the Hebrew word *môqêsh*. This word *môqêsh* can be translated as a *rope* or *noose that goes around the neck* or *a hook that is attached by piercing through the nose of a captive animal.*[56] Just like a noose around the neck or a hook in the nose, the fear of man is meant to control, humiliate, immobilize, pull or redirect anyone who falls subject to its power. With the fear of man comes tremendous social pressure to conform to the opinions and expectations of others.

When I studied anatomy and physiology back in my grad school days, I learned how vulnerable the human neck is to pain. An Achilles tendon caught in a snare would also be very vulnerable. In fact, it's safe to say that if you control someone's neck or Achilles heel, you would be able to pull them in any direction you please. The consequences of giving in to the fear of man can be just as devastating.

To follow Jesus is to pay what many in this world would consider to be the ultimate price, surrendering one's reputation and status to Him. We are to die to ourselves and pick up our cross on a daily basis, leaving anything and everything behind that contradicts His will, including our reputations. In order to do this, we must be freed from the opinions and expectations others place upon us.

> *And He was saying to them all, "If anyone wishes to come after Me,*
> *he must deny himself, and take up his cross daily and follow Me.*
>
> - Luke 9:23

To follow Jesus is to pay this price. It is called *the cost of discipleship*, and it involves dying to ourselves, our agendas and our reputations. We must be willing to lose and forsake anything and everything that contradicts His will and purpose for our lives. Surrendering to God means surrendering our desire to be accepted and to pick up our cross, every day.

Back in the early 1990's, when I lived in Florida, I used to visit a popular state park named "Ichetucknee Springs." Ichetucknee Springs is located about one hour and a half northwest of Gainesville, Florida. The name Ichetucknee is an Indian word designating a geographic formation of several crystal-clear limestone springs that erupt out of the earth and run into the Santa Fe River.

The thing that made Ichetucknee Springs so appealing to me, however, was its native wildlife, along with its cool, clear water. It was like looking into a crystal clear aquarium. There are hundreds of swimmers, snorkelers, scuba divers and sunbathers that frequent the springs each summer. One of my favorite activities in those days was to rent an old black tire from a roadside vendor to use as an inner tube and float downstream. It was so peaceful and relaxing because all you had to do was jump on the inner tube and allow the clear, cool current to do the rest of the work.

I remember my first time going down the Ichetucknee so vividly, seeing dozens of people floating downstream, enjoying the pristine scenery and the sunshine. Many of the tubers were so relaxed that they had fallen asleep or were at best semi-conscious, their eyes closed as they floated along. As we all know, *it takes no effort to go downstream with the current.*

Occasionally, I would notice that someone had fallen off their tube and was now stranded as they watched their empty tube glide away. The quiet, relaxing atmosphere would be interrupted as they shouted and hollered for someone to grab their tube before it disappeared around the bend. Startled, someone would paddle furiously to grab the empty tube and then begin the arduous journey back upstream against the flow of the current. Those going against the flow had to work extra hard.

I imagine this is what Jesus had in mind when he was talking in Matthew 6:13 about the wide, easy path. You don't have to do anything; you just get into your tube and *go with the flow* all of your life. Sitting peacefully and floating is all that is required. The current will do the rest.

There are multitudes of people floating downstream, going along with the flow. Most of them are ignorant of their final destination and oblivious of the direction the river of life is taking them. Following the crowd might seem quite normal and natural to many of us. It is only when we begin to realize what our final destination will be that we begin

114

to see the negative consequences of going with the flow.

The Apostle Paul warned the church at Ephesus of the powerful pull the world's system can exert on people: "And you were dead in your trespasses and sins, in which you formerly walked according to the course of this world, according to the prince of the power of the air, of the spirit that is now working in the sons of disobedience" (Ephesians 2:1-2).

People can easily find themselves in the mainstream of society, unknowingly influenced to conform to the forces of the culture around them. Being swept along by "the course of this world" they are caught in the gravitational pull of the majority and will comfortably flow in the same direction as the majority does. It is not until we fully realize the dangerous consequences of giving in to the course of this world that we begin to grasp the urgency to cast off the fear of man.

Six Symptoms of the Fear of Man

We do not want to be swept along by the pull of the fear of man or remain held captive to its control all of our lives. We want to be aware of this weapon that the enemy uses, so that we can overcome it and walk in freedom.

To help you identify the fear of man in your own life and to walk free from its crippling and life-inhibiting effects, I have identified six symptoms of its presence in a person's life. The list is not exhaustive, but it will suffice to give you an indication of when you or someone you know may be struggling with the fear of man.

1. Fear of Public Speaking

By definition, *glossophobia* is *an abnormal fear or dread of speaking in public*.[57] This is one of the main fears that people have, no matter how old they are. Surveys reveal that most people report their fear of public speaking ahead of their fear of snakes, fear of heights or even fear of death. The thought of giving a speech scares people and it doesn't matter if your audience is your family or friends, classmates or strangers. The thought of putting yourself on the line before others can be paralyzing and even crippling.

Why all this anxiety about public speaking? It might be because we are intuitively attuned to the fact that there is a lot at stake when we step out and put our selves, our appearances and our thoughts on public display. We are afraid that our performance could affect our reputation, social status and future happiness. Our perceived self-image and public standing is of paramount importance because it relates directly to our sense of security. Severe anxiety about speaking in public is a sure indicator that we are laboring under the fear of man.

Let me tell you how the Lord exposed the fear of man in my life. Believe it or not, over the years I have encountered a few individuals who have frightened me. More often, however, it has been the fear of the opinions of a group of people that possessed the capacity to frighten me more.

Back in my college days at Tennessee Tech, while on the football team, I was voted team captain my senior year. I enjoyed a good amount of athletic success and public exposure as a result of playing college football. Based on my sports exploits and my perceived circle of popularity, I believed that I had somehow finally earned the admiration of my peers. I had achieved this elusive thing called "popularity," or so I thought.

Immediately after I graduated, I re-enrolled in graduate school. It was at that time that I attended a Christian meeting on the campus, and surrendered my life to the Lordship of Jesus Christ. Overnight, the focus of my whole life changed. I no longer was concerned about the things that interested me before, like parties, sports or my popularity. Instead, I quickly developed a consuming passion to share the gospel of Jesus with other students. Little did I know that my precious public-image as a well-liked athlete and man about town would soon come crashing down to the ground.

The Christian ministry that I became involved with had a strong emphasis on evangelism as a normal part of a healthy Christian lifestyle. I was taught that sharing your faith with others was not reserved for ministers or missionaries. It was intended for every believer. This focus on evangelism was perfect for me, because that's exactly what my born-again heart wanted to do. I wanted to tell others about Jesus!

It was around this time that I started reaching out to members of my former football team about my life-changing encounter with Jesus Christ. On many occasions, my attempts to communicate my faith with my teammates were met with cool indifference. Their responses were something like, "I am happy for you, but that is not for me," or "Thanks, but I already have my own thing going with God."

Not only did they disregard my gospel presentation, but I began to be aware that rumors and whispers were circulating around about me. What was said was something along the lines of: "Ken's found religion now. He's just going through a phase. In a few months he will be back again, acting like the old Ken." But there was no doubt about the clear difference between my newly transformed life in Christ and my former lifestyle. My old football buddies could not avoid noticing the change.

Many of my old friends now conveniently avoided me. To be honest, I was feeling a bit rejected. These were the people who had once been my buddies and friends, my teammates. We had laughed together at parties, fought, bled and battled together on the football field. But now, I felt like the odd man out.

I certainly did not enjoy being shunned, but I knew that I had been significantly changed by the gospel, and I had a responsibility to tell others about it. I also knew that what God said and thought about me was more important than what others thought. But I still had a deep desire to be liked. I liked the approval of people, and I thought that being a football player would still give me credit in my friends' eyes. *God had other ideas.*

A few months later, the pastor of our campus ministry, a very likeable and positive guy named Doug, called a special meeting. Pastor Doug announced that he wanted the students to meet with him on the campus free speech area on a particular day and time in the coming week. He explained that we each needed to be prepared to share our salvation story and testify about how Jesus had changed our lives.

This free speech area happened to be located in the main quad, in the center of a busy campus thoroughfare where hundreds of students passed by or sat around eating their lunch. He encouraged us that this would be a "great opportunity" to be bold about our faith and to try our hand at open air preaching. I thought, "Wow, open air preaching in front of all those students. That sounds very scary, but also very exciting!"

I felt I was up for it. I assured Pastor Doug and the rest of our student group that I would be glad to attend the open air event and lend moral support to my fellow Christians. However, deep down on the inside of me, I was deeply conflicted about this "great opportunity." Even to me, a big, strong football player, standing up in a public place and talking about Jesus sounded like a huge risk, a risk that I thought I would never take.

As soon as I left the Christian meeting, excuses started entering my mind, reasons why I couldn't attend the event, or if I did, why I couldn't participate. The one big question echoing through my mind was: *"If I do this, what will people think of me?"* I started trying to justify why I was feeling this way. I wanted to build a case for my doubt and fear, as if they were credible.

I thought, "Isn't Christianity supposed to be something private, more of a personal thing? Can't I just live a good Christian life and be a positive role model? Won't people somehow just get the message without me having to say anything?" I was dealing with a severe case of the fear of man. I doubted the ability of God to show Himself strong on my behalf if I put my reputation on the line.

My anxiety only increased as the campus event drew nearer. I had conveniently conceived of my excuse for why I could not attend the open-air event. I reasoned that I had to study for a test that was scheduled to take place the following week. I tried to appease my feelings of fear by convincing myself that I was still a new Christian, a spiritual babe, and that there would be many opportunities in the future for me to tell others about Jesus Christ. I actually reasoned myself into deciding not to attend the event and to wait to share publicly until I was a more seasoned and mature Christian.

I cannot forget the dreadful feeling I had when that fateful day came. After my class ended, I drove by the main quad on campus where the open-air preaching was going to take place. It was lunchtime, and there were already hundreds of students starting to gather there. I hoped that no one would recognize my blue Audi Fox as I drove by. I felt a little like a traitor. It began to dawn on me that I was not driving home to study because I was concerned about my exam. *I was driving away from the opportunity to share my faith because I was ashamed.* I felt a gut wrenching sense of conviction settle over me. I could not shake it off. This continued to bother me deeply.

I arrived at my apartment and ate lunch. I consoled myself by thinking that I could at least pray for my friends as they did what I would not. I had my favorite place for prayer right there, which happened to be a big beanbag pillow.

I went into the den and flopped down and started trying to pray. After all, I really did want God to bless my friends and their open-air preaching. I did want God to help those Christians to be bold witnesses, while I stayed back and protected my precious reputation from any potential criticism or persecution.

As I tried to pray, it seemed as though my prayers were not even making it to the ceiling. I began feeling very guilty for being afraid. I realized that I was ashamed to even associate with other Christians in public!

Finally, I sensed the Lord speak directly to me: "What are you doing here?" He said. "I don't want your nervous prayers. *I want you to go out on that university campus and tell the world about how I changed your life!*"

Immediately the Scripture in Luke chapter 9 verse 26 came into my mind: "For whoever is ashamed of Me and My words, the Son of Man will be ashamed of him when He comes in His glory."

I realized at that moment that I was ashamed to be identified with Christ, and if I missed this opportunity, He would be ashamed to be identified with me.

Stinging with conviction, I finally took action. I drove back to campus and walked out onto that quad where, thankfully, the Christian band was still playing, now having drawn a small crowd. My plan was just to be there and help support the group by my presence, but the moment I walked up to the quad, Pastor Doug greeted me with an encouraging smile and said, "Hey Ken, I am glad you made it. We are about to get started, and I want you to go first."

I was totally terrified when I heard those words. I was scared. I could literally feel a big noose tightening around my neck. I was as fearful and caught up in my own insecurities as the Scripture verse which says, "The fear of man brings a snare" (Proverbs 29:25). I tried to hide how frightened I was to my Pastor.

There was no way out but to go for it. Again, my plan was to be short and sweet. As I stepped up onto the bench to begin giving my testimony, I saw some of my football teammates walk by. Then I saw a couple of professors that I highly regarded walk directly toward me. I wondered, "Will they ever even acknowledge me again?"

All of a sudden, I felt God's presence, and nothing mattered anymore. I knew that I was supposed to speak, no matter what. I opened my mouth and God filled it.

That day, when I stepped up onto that park bench in the middle of the quad in that crowded college campus, I received a major spiritual breakthrough. Not only was I able to give my testimony about how Jesus saved me, but I also experienced a tremendous weight being lifted off of my soul.

Before I stepped up onto that park bench to speak, my mouth was so parched that I did not even think I would be able to talk. I was tongue-tied, my knees trembled, and I was shaking in my shoes. But by the time I finished speaking, I felt exhilarated and emboldened about my Christian faith. That one single event of open-air preaching broke the fear of man over me, giving me a surge of divine confidence to speak in public about my Christian faith, which I have continued to do in various forums to this day.

This incident is what God used to release me to preach and teach publicly. What happened in those few minutes of open-air preaching was truly liberating. *I got totally set free from the fear of man!* Since that day I no longer care what others think of me when I am in obedience to God. That Scripture in Romans 8:31 is totally true: "If God be for us, who can be against us?"

I have to laugh now about that experience because I can totally see how paralyzing and pointless fear of what others think can be. I can also see how silly it would be for me to let another person's opinion of me prevent me from taking the truth of what Jesus Christ has done for me to the rest of the world.

2. A Tendency to Avoid Confrontation

To have healthy relationships it may be necessary to confront someone about an issue that needs to be addressed in their life. This could be with a spouse or family member, or with a co-worker or friend. Confrontation is one of the most difficult things we need to do. Many people avoid confrontation for fear that their relationship will be damaged.

Confrontation can often rub people the wrong way, no matter how considerately or professionally we go about it. That is why so many people avoid it altogether. Rather than confront the person directly, those who are battling the fear of man will often vent their frustrations by telling a third party about their relational "problems" (usually a perceived hurt or offense) and further complicate the issue.

Sometimes to avoid confrontation we try to deny that we are offended altogether. Denying that we are angry, annoyed or grieved about an issue, only prolongs the offense, layering it deeper into our emotional basements. Emotions that we stuff and deny will not disappear by our avoiding them.

These tactics of avoiding confrontation and denying we're offended is emotionally destructive. By adopting these and other avoidance methods, many Christians have stuffed their relational pain so far down inside, that meaningful conversation about their beliefs is no longer possible. They live superficially, guarding themselves from both the possibility of future pain or healing. The deception in this lifestyle is that these people sacrifice voicing their values and living by their convictions to remain safe relationally.

When people have hurt us, or when the people closest to us require our input to change and achieve their goals, we must not be afraid to lovingly address them with the issue, even if what we are saying can be taken in a negative way. Providing a safe, loving, face-to-face atmosphere when confronting is the best way to deal with an issue that needs resolution. This is also true when sharing and communicating the gospel.

The fear of man combined with the desire for self-preservation creates a force that urges us to run from confrontation, avoiding the maturation process, resulting in weak, unfruitful lives. Self-preservation can be a paralyzing disease that only masquerades as peace. Taking our faith to the front lines will require that we deal with any areas in our lives that are un-surrendered and dismantle all protective walls of excuses that we have constructed. "We are to grow up in all *aspects* into Him who is the head, *even* Christ" (Ephesians 4:15).

But what about being tolerant? Traditionally, *tolerance* has been defined as *the ability to bear up or endure*.[58] However, according to a more recent edition of Merriam Webster's Dictionary, the definition has morphed to include not only the *capacity to endure pain or hardship* but *a sympathy or indulgence for beliefs or practices different from or conflicting with one's own*.[59]

This expanded definition would suggest a notion of *accepting and coming into agreement with* something that is or was disagreeable to you or disparate to your personal believe system. The definition suggests that some sort of agreement has been entered into. In other words, a *compromise* has been made.

Modern *tolerance* is seen as a virtue to a culture that excuses itself from taking any responsibility to confront anything or anyone. It is an *evasion tactic*. This runaway notion of tolerance has muffled many Christians and discouraged many good men and women from speaking out. As authors David Kinnaman and Gabe Lyons point out:

An uncomfortably large segment of Christians would rather agree with people around them than experience even the mildest conflict. According to this perspective, it's never right to criticize people or their decision and lifestyles.[60]

However, avoiding confrontation by trying to become more tolerant is just another way of preferring to look out for one's own reputation, *rather than expressing real care or concern for someone else by telling them what they need to hear.*

Modern tolerance is not like the Christian virtue of forbearance. *Forbearance* is *the exercise of patience, long suffering and restraint of passions,*[61] not a compromise of standards to keep peace. Modern tolerance is an emotionalized excuse used to avoid having a meaningful and candid conversation, with the possibility of coming to a true understanding. In the end, it hurts everyone much more than telling the truth, because it denies the possibility of maturely coming to a resolution.

Practicing *modern tolerance* is a *form of self-preservation* and is a clear sign of the fear of man operating in one's life.

3. The Inability to Take an Unpopular Stand

Another reason people tend to avoid sharing their faith is because they do not want people to reject or dislike them. Very few people find pleasure in being labeled as an outsider or criticized by the majority for being "different." This inability to take an unpopular stand is known as the *fear of being rejected*, and it can be a powerful deterrent for speaking the truth.

When it comes to fears, the fear of rejection and the fear of man are a bit like Siamese twins. They tend to go together. They are phobias that *deify* public opinion.

It is important to emphasize that Jesus and His early followers were a radical minority that in many ways went directly against the religious and social trends of their day. Without a doubt, they knew what it was like to be unpopular. In fact, ten of the original twelve disciples were martyred because of their public stand for Christianity.

Jesus' disciples understood that sharing their faith was not an option. These are the words that Jesus had to say about this to His first followers:

> *Remember the word that I said to you, "A slave is not greater than his master. If they persecuted Me, they will also persecute you; if they kept My word, they will keep yours also. But all these things they will do to you for My name's sake, because they do not know the One who sent Me."*

> - John 15:20-21

Jesus also warned His disciples that there would be two categories of people consisting of the *many* and the *few*. From a spiritual perspective, the majority is not where you want to be.

> *Enter through the narrow gate; for the gate is wide and the way is broad that leads to destruction, and there are many who enter through it. For the gate is small and way is narrow that leads to life, and there are few who find it.*

> - Matthew 7:13-14

Notice that Jesus talked about two distinct pathways, two distinct entryways, and two distinct destinations. He warned His listeners to enter by the narrow gate. Why is this? Because the wide gate represents those on life's road who are caught up in the vanities of life, easily swept into the sea of pressing bodies. These people are distracted by the cares and the worries of the world comfortably living self-centered lives, taking no notice of their final destination.

Jesus strongly exhorted His listeners to choose the way that was narrow. This gate would be difficult to find, off the beaten road, its capacity much smaller. But its final destination would be life. It may not be the most popular. You may end up rejected and persecuted. But when you are on this path that leads to life, you are never alone (Matthew 28:20).

4. Telling Others What You Think They Want to Hear

This particular form of the fear of man goes beyond healthy social interaction by causing individuals to feel so insecure about themselves they will do almost anything to be accepted and feel loved. People like this become *man-pleasers*, trying to fulfill other people's expectations of them. Conforming our lives to meeting other people's expectations for us can be exhausting and simply impossible.

People who suffer from being man-pleasers have chosen to deny their own voice just to get approval. They can become codependent personalities, often attracted to more dominant personalities, who will gladly speak for them, thereby rescuing them from the natural maturation process.

Sadly, until these individuals decide to take responsibility for developing their own voice, and begin insisting on healthy relational boundaries, they will never come into their own strength of personality.

Back in my college days, I was asked by a student, "How do you like my new haircut?"

I was a freshman at the time and was eager to fit in, so when this young lady, who was accompanied by a group of her coed friends, asked me about her haircut, I just managed to blurt out, "Oh, I thinks it's cute."

I told her what she wanted to hear, even though I actually thought her new bowl haircut was kind of ugly compared to the long hair she had sported before. Basically, because I wanted to preserve my good standing with this young lady and with the group, I lied.

I am not suggesting that we need to be rude or insensitive to people. But this is an example of how the fear of man can take on the very subtle form of man-pleasing.

Trying to please people can also be a way of trying to advance ourselves. This is particularly true if the people we are trying to please have the ability to enrich or promote us. This type of man-pleaser is called a sycophant and is motivated out of selfish ambition and self-promotion. According to Webster's dictionary, a *sycophant* is *a flatterer, especially of great men, hence a deceiver; an impostor; a parasite.*[62]

As Christians motivated out of the fear of the Lord, we may have to take a public stand for biblical truths even though they may be unpopular or even offensive to others. We do not want to fall into the trap of serving our own personal interests by being a sycophant man-pleaser that bows to the consensus.

Isaiah saw clearly the condition of man:

"Stop regarding man, whose breath of life is in his nostrils; for why should he be esteemed?"

- Isaiah 2:22

God created man, not the other way around! Through this prophet, God cautioned His people not to overly revere human achievements or esteem human opinions.

The Apostle Paul also wrote to the Galatian church, "For am I now seeking the favor of men, or of God? Or am I striving to please men? If I were still trying to please men, I would not be a bondservant of Christ" (Galatians 1:10). He was definitely not afraid of what people thought of him or of his commitment to Christ. Paul was willing to be beaten, thrown into prison or even executed if God required it of him. By his own admission, he was now an unapologetic God-pleaser, and *not* a man-pleaser.

This dichotomy between pleasing God and pleasing men is what each and every Christian must face head-on if he or she desires to have the boldness to engage our contemporary society with the gospel.

5. A Peace-at-All-Costs Philosophy

There is a deep psychological need in every person to have a sense of security and peace. For example, I know that I sleep better at night when my doors are locked securely. Over the years I have had many security alarms installed to protect my possessions, not to mention the money I have spent on insurance plans. Somehow, as human beings, we

129

think doing these things will keep us safe and free from the storms of life, but true security comes from a life of faith and obedience to the Lord.

Instead of being willing to endure conflict and engage in the cultural battle head on, many Christians have succumbed to the temptation to be *passive*, thinking they can somehow broker a spiritual *détente* with the world.

One of the names given to Jesus in Scripture is "Prince of Peace" (Isaiah 9:6). How many times, for example, have you seen pictures of Jesus holding a little lamb on His lap, or maybe carrying one around his neck? These are my earliest memories of pictures of Jesus when I was a little boy at Baptist Sunday School. Jesus was portrayed as a gentle, smiling, compassionate shepherd, sweetly tending little lambs.

I must admit that this view of Jesus was comforting to my small boy's imagination. But later on in junior high, I had serious doubts about whether this Jesus would have made the cut to my school's football team, or withstood an attack from our neighborhood bully.

Have you ever seen some of the classical paintings depicting childlike angels flying around with wings? These cherubs are very cute and innocent looking, but the one thing they don't do is present a sense of God's power and authority. These distorted artistic portrayals of Jesus and Christianity send an incomplete message that Christianity is an impotent and docile religion.

"Gentle Jesus, meek and mild." Who wouldn't want to make such a Jesus a savior and a friend? Who could resist such a kind, understanding and harmless God?

Unfortunately for many, however, this portrayal of Jesus as passive is a distortion of the true character of Jesus. In biblical Christianity, the angels of God are described as warlike with brandished swords of flaming fire (Genesis 3:24). They are portrayed fighting off dark principalities in the heavenly realms (Daniel 10:13; Ephesians 6:12), and pouring out bowls of judgment upon unrepentant souls in the last days (Revelation 16).

Let us not be forgetful of the true nature of God Almighty as the Ancient of Days who will return to earth as a victorious conqueror to judge and wage war, riding on a white horse with eyes a flame of fire (Revelation 19:11-16).

Many sincere Christians believe the only example Jesus gave to us for dealing with the world was to be *very, very nice* and not offend them. Maybe if we are nice, loving and tolerant enough, people will want to become Christians? Maybe if our polite demeanors are enacted with enough smiles, the people around us will repent and bow their knee to Jesus. But is being polite and courteous even what God is asking for?

Most Christians are very aware that the Bible teaches things like compassion, gentleness, mercy and forgiveness. I thank God for these spiritual fruits and virtues. Jesus is the Prince of Peace, and as His followers we desire His peace to reign on earth, as well. But does this mean that the Christian response must be with an attitude of tolerance and universal forgiveness?

A peace-at-all-costs posture suggests that Christians should always be passive and ready to turn the other cheek, no matter what the situation. The favorite Scripture segment for a person of this persuasion is found in the Beatitudes in Matthew chapter five, where Jesus states that the peacemakers are blessed. He goes on to say that the meek are blessed as well.

Although it is true that we as Christians are called to be meek, and that it is also our duty to forgive each other even as Christ forgave us (Ephesians 4:32; Colossians 3:13), it would be a mistake to assume that Christianity is primarily docile and self-abasing. In this verse, the word *meekness* means something much different than our contemporary definition. In His meekness, Jesus has shown a greater power than displayed by any mighty army. Meekness is not weakness but is controlled strength. Meekness is submissiveness to the will of God.[63]

Was Jesus a man of controlled strength? Yes, He was. Jesus repeatedly demonstrated His self-control in His submission to the Father's will, including His choice to submit to dying on the cross as a criminal even though innocent. He subdued His flesh and endured the cross, despising the shame, in obedience to His Father's will (Matthew 26:39).

Did Jesus at times exhibit anger? Yes, He made a whip and violently overturned the money changers' tables, driving them out of the temple in righteous anger in the Gospel of Mark (11:15). It was Jesus who became agitated and rebuked the scribes, lawyers and Pharisees, calling them "a brood of vipers" (Matthew 3:7). In fact, Jesus even informed His followers that His Kingdom was suffering violence and that those who are violent take it by force.

> *From the days of John the Baptist until now the kingdom of heaven suffers violence, and violent men take it by force.*
>
> - Matthew 11:12

The mistaken notion that Jesus was only a soft-spoken, introverted type is a completely false view of the Messiah. The reality is that Jesus possessed all the attributes associated with mercy, grace and forgiveness, along with the attributes of righteous anger, godly indignation and holy wrath towards evildoers and unrepentant sinners.

True peace will never be achieved by passively adapting to the world's system. God has not called us to compromise our Christian values just to quiet the accusations of the opposition. I might step on a few toes here, but passivity can be just a ruse for laziness.

6. Indecisiveness

People who struggle with the fear of man are also very often indecisive. As James, the head of the church in Jerusalem and brother to Jesus writes,

> For the one who doubts is like the surf of the sea, driven and tossed by the wind. For that man ought not to expect that he will receive anything from the Lord, being a double-minded man, unstable in all his ways.
>
> - James 1:6-8

Double-minded people are afraid of what others will say or think about them if they make the wrong decision. This literally means that they are of two minds: one voice often being that of doubt and fear, the other voice of truth and reason.

Because these people listen to two voices, they are unstable, trying to go in two directions at the same time. They take two steps in one direction, then doubt themselves and go back two, sometimes three, steps in the other direction. Their indecisiveness is followed by more anxiety and doubt, which in turn generates still more fear, condemnation and instability.

Being double-minded is not only crippling, but it is also mentally tormenting. "Anxiety in a man's heart weighs it down" (Proverbs 12:25).

God, however, did not create mankind to be oppressed with fear. He intended for us to be filled with His Spirit:

> *For God has not given us a spirit of fear, but of power and of love and of a sound mind.*
>
> - 2 Timothy 1:7 (NKJV)

God has divinely provided us a way to be free from the fear of man and to counter the flow of the world's influence. God desires that we reject the spirit of fear and choose to receive His Spirit of power, love, and a sound mind.

The Solution: The Fear of the Lord

The fear of the Lord is the most powerful guiding force or principle for a person's life. Walking in a healthy, reverential fear of the Lord will keep one's steps in line with the will of God.

The Book of Proverbs, one of the greatest collections of wisdom literature of all time, records: "In the fear of the Lord there is strong confidence, and His children will have refuge. The fear of the Lord is a fountain of life, that one may avoid the snares of death" (Proverbs 14:26-27). "The fear of the Lord is to hate evil; pride and arrogance and the evil way and the perverted mouth, I hate" (Proverbs 8:13).

Job, who greatly feared the Lord as described in the book which bears his name, was prompted by his fear of the Lord to turn away from evil (Job 1:1).

In Psalm 128:1, the person who fears the Lord is described as walking in happiness and blessings. Satisfaction and wealth are also promised for those who walk in godly fear (Psalm 112:1-8). Solomon contrasts the person who fears the Lord with the wicked: "Although a sinner does evil a hundred *times* and may lengthen his *life*, still I know that it will be well for those who fear God, who fear Him openly" (Ecclesiastes 8:13).

Scripture promises a host of other benefits for those who fear God and keep His commandments. The fear of the Lord brings goodness from God (Psalm 31:19), provision for needs (Psalm 34:9), overshadowing mercy (Psalm 103:11), protection (Psalm 33:18–19), and the promise of desires fulfilled (Psalm 145:19).

So how is the fear of the Lord to be attained? Begin first by seeking the Lord and asking Him for it. God will graciously give us the fear of the Lord, while at the same time enabling us to combat the paralyzing influences of fear that we are facing as we choose instead to put our trust in the Lord.

Bold as a Lion

In light of this, you might be wondering how on earth you are ever going to muster the courage to defend your faith, let alone advance it. The great news about standing with God is you don't have to rely on your own strength or willpower. Through Christ's blood, God not only purchased for you the forgiveness of your sins but, also granted those who receive Him to be made righteous or simply *brought into right standing with Him.* When God looks at us, He sees the blood of His Son, clothing us with His gift of righteousness. This is called *imputed righteousness.*

> *The wicked flee when no one is pursuing, but the righteous are bold as a lion.*
> - Proverbs 28:1

Knowing that we are in right standing with God gives us confidence, making us bold as a lion whenever we speak to anyone about our Great Savior. More than that, He has graciously given us His Holy Spirit to empower us to be witnesses (Acts 1:8).

➤ Rule #4: Speak with Confidence.

Once a Christian realizes that he or she has been given the "righteousness of God in Christ Jesus" (2 Corinthians 5:21), the fear of death and the fear of man will no longer have any legal hold on their life.

In Christ, there is no longer anything to fear regarding man's opinions. The worst that anyone can do to a believer is to ridicule, persecute or perhaps attempt to kill him. But for the believer, even death is no longer to be feared:

> *"Where, O death, is your victory? Where, O death, is your sting?"*
> *The sting of death is sin, and the power of sin is the law. But thanks*
> *be to God! He gives us the victory through our Lord Jesus Christ.*
> - 1 Corinthians 15:55-57 (NIV)

As believers, we probably won't win many popularity contests with the world's system. Then again, that is not our primary concern, is it? "If you were of the world, the world would love its own; but because you are not of the world, but I chose you out of the world, because of this the world hates you" (John 15:19).

If the world persecuted and crucified Jesus for speaking the truth, we shouldn't be surprised for being rejected and persecuted for the same thing. The opposition that we face in this world is because of the truth that we carry. Being sensitive and winsome to non-believers is commendable, but it will be the truth, not our winning smiles, that will set people free: "And you will know the truth, and the truth will make you free" (John 8:32).

Deliverance from Fear

The following Psalm is a beautiful picture of how God delivers His people from the bondage of fear. It is also how I personally received victory over the fear of man in my own life. I believe it can do the same for you.

O, magnify the LORD with me, and let us exalt His name together.
I sought the LORD, and He answered me, and delivered me from
all my fears.

- Psalm 34:4

Remember, "The wicked man flees when no one is pursuing, but the righteous are as bold as a lion" (Proverbs 28:1). Now is the time to get set free from the fear of man. Now is the time to seek the Lord's help. You can have that noose of fear taken from around your neck that has been choking the life of God out of you. It's time for you today to put your trust in Almighty God and repent for fearing what people think about you, and for submitting to a spirit of fear in your life. Instead, God wants you to trust Him to make you fearless concerning the things of the Kingdom. God wants to deliver you from the spirit of fear. I encourage you to pray this prayer aloud.

Prayer of Deliverance

Lord Jesus, I asked You to forgive me for fearing the opinions of man over Your opinion. I now know that fearing people and what they think will cause me to be ensnared and paralyzed by the enemy. Instead, I choose to fear You, God and believe what Your word says about me. I repent for trying to be popular just to fit in with the crowd. I repent for trying to protect my reputation at the expense of shrinking back from being godly and proclaiming God's truth to others. I am no longer ashamed of the gospel. What matters most is what You think about me, not what other people think. I give You my reputation. I choose to fear God more than man. I ask You in the name of Jesus, to take this noose from around my neck. Thank You, Jesus, for setting me free by the power of Your blood to be a bold witness for Christ in this generation. Amen!

CHAPTER SIX

Boots on the Ground

The meaning of the military term *boots on the ground* is generally understood as indicating *military forces deployed and ready for military conflict.*[64] As Christ's disciples, we are to make sure that we daily live our lives ready to be deployed out into the world. Sometimes this literally requires people traveling to a specific location and directly interacting with the people of that region.

➤ Rule #5: Think and Act Strategically.

There is a strategic nature behind Christian missions, which is very similar to a military campaign. To have a boots on the ground mentality requires that believers are mobilized and sent to cities and nations specifically to take territory, where they can establish a beachhead of operations to continue to carry out the task of Christian engagement in that area.

Most missiologists call this procedure *church planting.* Several studies have shown that one of the best ways to evangelize a city is to establish a new church in that area. Interestingly, the term *evangelical,* dating back to the sixteenth century, is used with reference to Catholic writers who wished to revert back to more biblical beliefs and practices.

As we understand it now, evangelicalism centers on four key

principles: the authority and sufficiency of Scripture; the uniqueness of redemption through the death of Christ on the cross; the need for personal conversion; and the necessity, propriety and urgency of evangelism.[65]

Again we must be reminded, Christians have been given the power of the Holy Spirit to be God's witnesses through the whole world (Acts 1:8). Jesus has commissioned His followers to go and make disciples of all nations (Matthew 28:19). Paul proclaims that we are ambassadors of the Kingdom wielding the message of reconciliation whereby we persuade men (2 Corinthians 5:17-20).

We have been given a divine mission. This is why evangelical Christians call the territory assigned to them the mission field. Missionaries have an assignment that they must carry out if they want to accomplish their specific mission.

The Paul Apostle wrote that people, through observing the created order, can surmise that there is a God, and still refuse to acknowledge Him as God (Romans 1:19-20). The knowledge of God that can be inferred through observation is not sufficient for salvation without the gospel presentation. Paul further writes that the contents of the gospel come only through a human messenger: "How can they hear without a preacher" (Romans 10:14c)?

In His sovereignty, God has ordained the gospel transmission to be communicated person-to-person. D. L. Moody concurred when he said, "If this world is going to be reached, I am convinced that it must be done by men and women of average talent."[66]

Time to Mobilize

One day before Renee and I moved our family to New Zealand back in 1999, we were driving along in our Chevy Suburban listening to a CD about being a "light to the nations." At one point, a very passionate female intercessor began to pray for the nations around the world. She ended by asking, "God, release those laborers with a lifetime call, who are fully-funded, into the harvest."

Renee and I, amazed at her clarity, nodded our heads, whispering, "Yes, Lord. Send *them*."

We both began to cry, feeling a real burden for the lost people of the world. We were overcome by the presence of God while we drove through Tennessee listening to this anointed prayer going forth.

At the time, our ministry in America was going quite well. I was traveling around the country ministering evangelistically. I was a part of a nation-wide athletic ministry that served athletes at the professional and collegiate level, as well as serving as the dean of a Bible school and leadership institute.

During this same period of time, I also had a very troubling dream. In the dream I saw myself in a hotel room lying in a bed. As I looked up from the bed I saw a young child, a toddler, sitting precariously on the ledge of an open window. The hotel was in a high-rise building and my room seemed to be on the top story. I knew instinctively that the child was in great danger and about to fall out of the window. In my dream, I was desperately trying to get out of bed to reach the child before he fell. The next thing I knew, I was fully awake, sitting up in my bed. I very seldom remember any of my dreams, but on this occasion I knew this was a dream from God. I just didn't know what it meant.

After praying over this dream and sharing it with our ministry elders, we felt strongly that this young child sitting in the window and falling in my dream represented a young church plant that I had helped establish in 1988 in Auckland, New Zealand, which the pastor had decided to close down shortly after.

It wasn't long before Renee and I knew that our "Yes, Lord. Send *them.*" Had become, "Yes, Lord. Send *us!*" We were the answer to the prayer that this woman had prayed concerning sending missionaries to the nations. God was asking us to actually move overseas to help take the gospel to these precious people in New Zealand and to re-establish that original church plant.

Within a few short months, in the fall of 1999, we were sent out by our ministry to relocate to Auckland, New Zealand to birth the new church and serve as Regional Directors in the South Pacific. A little over a decade later, we had seen the Lord stablish many church plants in New Zealand and Australia that had resulted from our willingness to answer His call.

In 2012, after much prayer and fasting, we sold our home in Auckland, gave away our cars, packed our belongings and answered the call to move to Brisbane, Australia, to establish another new church plant, also in the South Pacific region. Because we were in our fifties, everyone thought that we were taking a huge risk to start over again. Believe me, I was very aware that I was no longer the young buck that I had been in my thirties and forties, but deep inside, I knew that if Abraham could trust God to give him a son at his ripe old age of 99, pioneering a new church plant in my fifties would not be too big of a problem for Him.

I am now thrilled and relieved to say that God *was* in it and He did indeed grace our efforts. We left that beautiful church in the hands of a dear son in the Lord, Neli Atiga, two years later when we returned back to the USA. Today, the South Pacific region has numerous Every Nation Churches and Ministries in New Zealand, Australia, and the islands of Fiji and Papua New Guinea.

Opportunity Knocks

Opportunity is missed by most people because it is dressed in overalls and looks like work.

- Thomas Edison[67]

There is a statue in Greece that is called "Opportunity." According to Greek legend, this statue represents the youngest son of the Greek god Zeus. It serves as a vivid portrayal of how opportunity looks.

In this Greek statue, opportunity is depicted as a young man with long locks of hair hanging down from his forehead. The backside of the statue's head has no hair. This is to indicate that opportunity can only be grasped as he approaches. Conversely, once opportunity has passed you by, there is no chance to grab hold of him because the back of his head is totally bald.[68]

The Greek word for *opportunity* is kairŏs. *Kairŏs* literally means *the suitable time, the right moment, the opportune time.*[69] Planting our first church in Auckland, New Zealand was definitely a *kairŏs* moment for Renee and me.

I had gone to the airport to pick up our friends Kirk and Leslie Henderson and their young family, who were just arriving from America to join our church plant in New Zealand. While waiting for the Henderson family to come through customs, I saw a young and athletic Samoan man standing in the waiting area.

I felt that the Lord wanted me to talk to him, so I went over and introduced myself. It turned out this guy was a rugby player named Saita and was in fact very active in sports. We had an immediate connection, having been an all-American university football player and having worked extensively with college and professional athletes during my ministry career up to that time. Saita and I talked for a long while and exchanged phone numbers.

Later that week I called Saita and invited him and his wife, Novalene, over for dinner. After our airport encounter, Saita had somehow gotten the impression that I was some kind of American sports agent scouting for the NFL. He thought I was on the lookout to recruit talent in New Zealand. To this day, I am not sure how he got that idea. Maybe it was because we had talked about sports. In any case, when I called him over to have a Bible study and dinner at my home, he assumed that I was trying to recruit him to play in the NFL.

When Saita and Novalene came over for dinner with their two young boys that fateful night, Renee and I shared our testimonies with them and presented the gospel. Amazingly, they both received Jesus. It was only after they gave their lives to Christ that Saita revealed his real motivation for accepting the dinner invitation. He had come to my home hoping to negotiate and sign a big, fat, pro contract! It's very funny to think about it now, but it's true. Sometimes our wrong motives can be exactly what God uses to get His desired results.

God knew what He was doing. Saita may not have gotten a NFL

contract, talented athlete though he was, but what he did get was worth a whole lot more. He and his family were destined to be miraculously apprehended by God's grace.

A few weeks later, Novalene was at our home again with their six-year-old son, Dujean. As it turned out, Dujean suffered from a rare form of juvenile leukemia. In contrast to his dad, a large, hulking man, he was a small, sickly boy who had not grown much over the previous two years. Dujean was on a lot of medication and under constant doctor's observation and care.

Standing in the foyer of our home, Novalene and Saita asked us to pray for their son because they were convinced that God could heal him. The next week they took Dujean to the medical specialist for an examination, and to the doctor's amazement, Dujean's leukemia was totally gone! The doctors were skeptical at first, but after a few months, removed the I.V. apparatus that had been embedded in his arm for treatments.

Dujean, miraculously healed by God, immediately began to put on weight and grow at a very rapid rate. Dujean and his brother Lamar have played professional rugby in Australia. To the glory of God, his leukemia has never returned! Saita and Novalene are currently church members in our Every Nation Church in Brisbane.

Another *kairŏs* moment comes to mind. In 2012, a few days after arrival in Australia, I received an email from a young lady, a member of our Every Nation church family in Manila, Philippines. She had been praying for an Every Nation Church to be planted in Brisbane. She emailed me to tell us that Renee and I were the answer to her prayers.

I had never met this woman before in my life, but she gave me the number of an Australian man she had met in the Philippines the year before that she had witnessed to about Jesus, named Michael, and lived in Brisbane. She gave me his details and asked me to give him a call.

I called and invited Michael to stop by our home the following Thursday for lunch. That day I was able to explain the gospel more fully to him and lead him to repent from sin and put his faith in Christ. A week later he was water baptized and filled with the Spirit. He is now a strong Christian leader in our Every Nation church in Brisbane. Coincidentally, he recently got married to the beautiful Filipino woman who had witnessed to him over a year earlier in Manila. Her name is Alma.

Another opportune moment literally came knocking at my door in that same house in Brisbane. On this particular Friday evening we were praying for believers who had been isolated from the Church to return to Christ. Honestly, it was a little startling to have our prayers answered so quickly by a strong knock on the front door. We all stopped praying, wondering who it could be. I opened the door to see a man standing there looking like a member of a motorcycle gang. He wore a Fu Manchu mustache and beard. His hair was slicked back behind his ears, as he asked in his strong Aussie accent, "Hey mate, is there a prayer meeting here tonight?"

I said the only thing I could say, "Yes, there is." I proceeded to invite him into my living room. I introduced myself and the others to him and asked him to share a bit about himself. His name was Alex and I found out that he had heard from a friend that there was a prayer meeting going on at this address on this particular Friday night, so he had decided to check it out.

As Alex walked in, I noticed that on the front of both of his shins were large, colorful tattoos. On his right leg was a picture of the devil holding a pentagram. And on the back of his left leg there was a tattoo of Jesus hanging on the cross. I asked him about the tattoos later, and he told me that the tattoo on his right leg depicted his life while he was following Satan, whereas the tattoo of Jesus on his left leg portrayed when he had decided to give Jesus a try.

I couldn't believe it. We had been praying for God to send us people in the city who were struggling in their faith or had backslidden away from God! As far as appearances could tell - and I teased him about this later - he fit the description perfectly. I invited Alex over to my home for dinner the next evening, where he informed me that he was just about to turn his back on God and Christianity to return to his former lifestyle of drugs, drinking and womanizing.

Thankfully, that night I was able to counsel and pray with Alex. The next few months Alex met with our men's group every Wednesday morning, reading the Bible and getting mentored. Alex is now actively committed to ministering to the poor, imprisoned and homeless.

Life is full of opportunities. We can ignore them as they pass us by, or we can grab hold of them and make an eternal impact on the life of someone else. Thinking back about people like Saita, Michael, and Alex I am so glad God gave me the chance to meet these men and seize the opportunity to share with them about Christ.

The Power of One

There is a temptation in today's culture to think that "bigger is better." It is only too easy to think that one or two people can't really make much of a difference in the grand scheme of things and that the little decisions that we make each day are of little or no value. We often believe these false assumptions, even if we don't say them aloud. But just the opposite is true. Great world-changing events usually emerge from small, insignificant beginnings.

For example, we know that in the beginning of His ministry Jesus selected twelve ordinary men to be His disciples. These fishermen, farmers and tax collectors had no exceptional giftings or pedigrees, yet, through them Jesus was able to impact and upset the whole world with the gospel (Acts 17:6).

While I was ministering on the University of Auckland, a Christian club invited me to speak to their group of about 15-20 people. I decided to accept their invitation just to be nice and do them a favor. To be honest, I didn't put much stock in this small gathering. To my amazement, several students prayed to receive Christ.

At that meeting, there was a young Samoan student named Jarrett, a former all-star rugby player. Jarrett had suffered a career-ending knee injury. Prior to that injury, he had high hopes of playing professional rugby and was well on his way to achieving that goal. His injury changed everything.

Jarrett had a brother named Nathan, an atheist, who had attended our campus outreach a few weeks earlier and had surrendered his life to Christ. He was now constantly talking about Jesus to everyone. Jarrett could not deny the amazing change he now saw in his brother. After that small group meeting, Jarrett found his way to our Saturday-night service and was gloriously saved. He not only became a Christian but soon joined our campus ministry.

Over the next few years, Jarrett became equipped through our Bible school and became a full-time campus missionary at the University of Auckland. During his time in Auckland, Jarrett was responsible for dozens of students coming to know Jesus. Today he and his wife, Nicole, have planted a new church in Fiji, reaching out to students of the University of the South Pacific in that island nation. Looking back at the impact that Jarrett's life has made, I am so glad I didn't blow off the opportunity to speak to what appeared to be a small, insignificant group.

When our actions intersect with God's providential plan, there are eternal consequences. We have opportunities almost every day to talk to people about God. Our personal willingness to be ready and available for the Master to use us is a daily challenge for all Christians everywhere. We are to voluntarily engage the world with the gospel, as God's boots on the ground. Unfortunately, many Christians marginalize the biblical idea of prioritizing one's life to impact others for eternity until after they achieve their own personal goals. This is especially true in our generation where self-fulfillment and hedonism dominate most people's thinking.

For the love of Christ controls us, having concluded this, that one died for all, therefore all died; and He died for all, so that they who live might no longer live for themselves, but for Him who died and rose again on their behalf.

- 2 Corinthians 5:14-15

In contrast to this, the Apostle Paul reminds us about the emphasis of King David's life, "For David, after he had served the purpose of God in his own generation, fell asleep, and was laid among his fathers and underwent decay" (Acts 13:36).

David *chose* to serve the purpose of God in his own generation. Wow. What a powerful epitaph to mark the accomplishments of one's life. That would be the inscription that I would like to have written on my tombstone.

Living a full life is not just about the enjoyment of its passage or the quality of one's life here on earth. It's about fully engaging in God's purposes. What highlights a Christian's life as meaningful is not just the succession of moments in that life, but the significance of those moments.

God uses our simple, seemingly insignificant acts of obedience to engage people with the gospel, producing an amazing ripple effect that transfers to future generational blessings.

Commit to the Lost

In the 1994 blockbuster movie *Forrest Gump*, actor Tom Hanks is cast in the lead role as Forrest, a developmentally disabled child growing up in the deep South in the 1960's and 70's.

Even though the odds were stacked against Forrest, he nevertheless has a remarkable life through a series of accidental coincidences. The movie depicts him in many iconic historical events such as playing college football for Bear Bryant at the University of Alabama, winning the Medal of Honor in the Vietnam War, playing in China on the All-American ping-pong Team as part of President Nixon's diplomacy program, and eventually making his fortune in the shrimp business.

One day Forrest asks his mother, played by Sally Fields, "Mama, what's my destiny?" It is the simple-minded Forrest Gump's quest for purpose that drives him to overcome and accomplish so much.

If only the answer to Forrest's question were as straightforward as his drive for it. By the end of the movie, his lovable innocence and resilient friendship with his beloved Jenny convince us that human life has value.

Just as in the movie, everyone will eventually ask the four essential philosophical questions of: *origin, meaning, morality* and *destiny*.

Origin addresses the question, Where did I come from?

Meaning addresses the question, What is the purpose of my life, and why am I here?

Morality addresses the question, How am I meant to behave and interact with other people and the world while I am here?

Destiny addresses the question, Where am I going?

These are the primary questions of mankind. Does life happen by chance or by destiny? As such, these questions are perfect starting points for a conversation about the gospel.

Ultimately, the answers to these questions lead to recognition of divine purpose individually and corporately. We must understand that our lives and relationships are to be formed around God's overarching purpose to reach and disciple the lost.

Renee and I regularly receive compliments on the spiritual health of our marriage and our children. I would love to pat myself on the back and take credit for the grace of God that has kept us through all of the trials that we have faced as believers, but the main reason that our marriage and our family have stayed healthy is because we have cooperated with God's agenda to put His desires above our own. We have done this by prioritizing our lives by putting: our relationship with God first, then our marriage relationship, followed by our family relationships, and then by making ourselves available to reach out to others, especially the lost.

Many marriages and families are so inwardly focused that they miss the opportunity of hosting a ministry gathering in their home and seeing lives transformed. They experience contention, complaining and strife, instead of the love, peace and joy that the Holy Spirit brings when He is honored first. Doesn't James say, "For where envy and self-seeking exist, confusion and every evil thing are there" (James 3:16 NKJV)?

As we have prioritized the Kingdom of God in our lives as a family, blessings have overflowed into our children's lives in multiple ways, amazing scholarships and sports opportunities just to name a few.

Understanding our created purpose results in increased productivity and fruitfulness, bringing greater glory to the Father. "My Father is glorified by this, that you bear much fruit, and so prove to be My disciples" (John 15:9).

While we were living in Auckland, I would travel back and forth from New Zealand to the island nation of Samoa. We were trying to establish a new Bible training school and leadership institute there. Our church in Auckland was responsible to fly our New Zealand teachers every two weeks to Samoa to teach and train the Samoan students in the capital city of Apia.

The cost of underwriting airline flights to and from Samoa for the year was high. Our ministry spent a considerable amount of time, money and energy to run this Samoan Bible school from Auckland. Although this endeavor was challenging, it was also rewarding. We saw many lives changed by the gospel.

Someone once asked me, "Why do you go to all this trouble to establish a Bible school in a far-away place like Samoa?" I replied, "I wouldn't do it for anybody else but Jesus!" Jesus is the reason! That's not just a slogan to say around Christmas time. Whenever we have God's perspective and encounter hardship, our trial becomes an act of gratitude to honor God. There comes a time in every believer's journey where we understand the great price God had to pay to redeem us from our sin. Anything He asks of us is as nothing next to His great sacrifice.

Because of God's great mercy and forgiveness, we can obey; and indeed, we are obligated to do so. No request that the Lord may make of us is off-limits. To care for what Jesus cares about is our greatest way to identify with Him and love Him through our service.

Count the Cost

Truth carries with it confrontation. Truth demands confrontation; loving confrontation, but confrontation nevertheless.
    - Francis Schaeffer[70]

In their book *Transformational Church*, Ed Stetzer and Thom Rainer point out that "growth for the church and growth of the individual believer occur when we move 'out' by participating in God's mission."[71]

Many Christians are reluctant to share their faith in any situation. Imagine if encountering persecution and public hostility were a staple part of our presentation of the gospel. Would we present the gospel truth no matter what personal repercussions we might face? It's difficult to say how many contemporary Christians would answer the call to engage their culture if, like Paul, they knew beforehand about the many hardships and trials they would face. I fully understand that most Christians are not specifically called to walk in Paul's footsteps or to emulate his ministry call. That doesn't diminish the reality that contemporary Christians who choose to be faithful to the Great Commission may indeed suffer hostility, even persecution for their faith, much as Paul did.

If modern day believers ever suffer persecution for their commitment to Jesus, they will find themselves in very good company. According to Paul, those who really want to live godly lives will suffer persecution (2 Timothy 3:12). However, we should not lose heart. "Many are the afflictions of the righteous, but the Lord delivers him out of them all" (Psalm 34:19).

Therefore I am well content with weaknesses, with insults, with distresses, with persecutions, with difficulties, for Christ's sake; for when I am weak, then I am strong.

- 2 Corinthians 12:10

It is more than possible that the God who has prepared the gospel for all people has also prepared the people who hear it to be receptive to it. In fact, God confirms over and over again throughout Scripture that He has prepared the hearts of the Gentiles to receive the good news (Luke 2:30-32). The prophet Isaiah writes that those who walk in darkness, the unsaved Gentiles, will see a great light (Isaiah 9:2).

It's time for you to evaluate your willingness to be involved in engaging your world with the gospel. Being placed front and center means a person can no longer excuse himself from carrying out the Master's cause. The question God posed to the Prophet Isaiah centuries ago in

Isaiah 6:8 is still echoing through eternity to believers: "Whom shall I send, and who will go for Us?"

It is imperative that all believers be willing and available to be carriers of the gospel message, couriers of the good news. We must demonstrate a focused availability to be God's witnesses.

Our response should be, as Isaiah's was: "Here am I. Send me!" And the Lord will then say, as He did in Isaiah 6:9, "Go, and tell this people."

CONCLUSION

The Ministry of Reconciliation

God has empowered each of us, as believers, to be His representatives. "Now all these things are from God, who reconciled us to Himself through Christ and gave us the ministry of reconciliation" (2 Corinthians 5:18). You and I have each been given a precious gift: *the ability to reconcile people to Christ!* In other words, the ability to do the work of the evangelist is resident within each one of us, waiting to be activated.

Someone once said, "Your greatest ability is your availability." *Have you made yourself available to be used by God?* Have you said, "Yes, Lord, send me?" The good news is that any believer can learn a few simple strategies for sharing the gospel with those around them. You don't have to be an anointed preacher to take up the cause of Christ. You just need to be willing to roll up your sleeves and work! "But you, be sober in all things, endure hardship, do the work of the evangelist, fulfill your ministry" (2 Timothy 4:5).

It is true that doing the ministry of the evangelist is work, but it is an amazingly rewarding work. What a privilege it is to witness the new birth process when someone fully surrenders their life to Christ Jesus as their Lord and Savior. Your life will be greatly impacted as you spend the following few weeks and months establishing biblical foundations in their life and teaching them to obey God's word. I have never regretted the personal investment that is required to lead and disciple a new believer in Christ.

Bearing fruit in evangelism begins with being intimate with Jesus. "Abide in Me, and I in you. As the branch cannot bear fruit of itself unless it abides in the vine, so neither can you unless you abide in Me. I am the vine, you are the branches; he who abides in Me and I in him, he bears much fruit, for apart from Me you can do nothing" (John 15:4-5).

Evangelism is motivated out of a recognition of our complete dependency upon the Holy Spirit to guide and lead through each encounter. "For all who are led by the Spirit of God are the children of God" (Romans 8:14 NLT).

Introducing someone to Jesus is a process that involves learning to work with the Holy Spirit and His timing. Paul reminds us that we are co-laborers:

> *What then is Apollos? And what is Paul? Servants through whom*
> *you believed, even as the Lord gave opportunity to each one. I planted,*
> *Apollos watered, but God was causing the growth. So then neither*
> *the one who plants nor the one who waters is anything, but God who*
> *causes the growth. Now he who plants and he who waters are one; but*
> *each will receive his own reward according to his own labor.*
>
> - 1 Corinthians 3:5-8

When it comes to evangelism, on occasions I have heard Christians try to exempt themselves of this responsibility by saying, "That's not my ministry calling," or "I'm not comfortable talking to strangers about my personal beliefs." While I agree and admit that individuals do have different temperaments, callings, and giftings, I still firmly believe that every Christian has been given the ministry of reconciliation and is to participate in evangelism in one form or another.

You may not be called as a fulltime evangelist or vocational minister, but there are still many respectful and considerate ways in which you can share your faith with your friends or colleagues without compromising the truth. The way each person goes about this may look differently, but the fact that we are each to commit ourselves to this work is inseparable from the Great Commission.

Perhaps you have heard someone say, "Oh, I just go around planting seeds," or "I just water the seeds." That may sound sweet and kind, but Jesus, after revealing His identity to the woman at the well, exhorted His disciples to think much differently. He told them to labor in faith, expecting to reap where others had sown:

> Do you not say, 'There are yet four months, and then comes the harvest'? Behold, I say to you, lift up your eyes and look on the fields, that they are white for harvest. Already he who reaps is receiving wages and is gathering fruit for life eternal; so that he who sows and he who reaps may rejoice together. For in this case the saying is true, 'One sows and another reaps.' I sent you to reap that for which you have not labored; others have labored and you have entered into their labor.
>
> - John 4:35-38

Pray for Open Hearts

Prayer is much more powerful than human persuasion can ever

be. It is so important to the evangelist's endeavor that Paul instructed his young disciple Timothy to pray for the stability of the government in which he resided, so that it would remain suitable for Christian living and the spread of the gospel message:

> *I urge that entreaties and prayers, petitions and thanksgivings, be made on behalf of all men, for kings and all who are in authority, so that we may lead a tranquil and quiet life in all godliness and dignity. This is good and acceptable in the sight of God our Savior, who desires all men to be saved and to come to the knowledge of truth.*
>
> - 1 Timothy 2:1-6

The Apostle Paul also urged the Corinthians to recognize the true situation of all unbelievers, "In whose case the god of this world has blinded the minds of the unbelieving so that they might not see the light of the gospel of the glory of Christ, who is the image of God" (2 Corinthians 4:4).

Evidently, Paul saw a direct connection between prayer and the openness to receive the gospel. Without prayer, people will continue to believe the lies that have shaped and surrounded them, remaining in their spiritual darkness eternally separated from God. Because this is the case, we must be intentional to pray before we engage people with the gospel. Pray that God will direct you to people who will be receptive to your message.

As Matthew 16:19 and 18:18 tell us, "Whatever you bind on earth shall have been bound in heaven, and whatever you loose on earth shall have been loosed in heaven." So when you pray, be specific and walk in the authority that God has given you over principalities, earthly and heavenly. Don't just strike out blindly.

Also, do not discount the power of praying with someone after you have shared the gospel. Most people will not turn down a sincere and well-meaning request to pray for them. I have encountered atheists and agnostics who have gladly invited me to pray for them, regardless of whether or not they believed in God or accepted my message.

Praying for people after sharing the gospel has also given me an open door to continue the relationship. It not only endears you to them as someone who genuinely cares, but the presence of the Holy Spirit manifests tangibly bringing undeniable peace and comfort.

It is essential that the gospel presenter be familiar with various Bible texts and apologetic answers to deal with objections, however, even if a believer is well-equipped with Scriptural knowledge and evangelistic strategies, without the power of prayer, the evangelistic efforts will fall short. Only the Spirit and power of God can soften hard hearts and transform lives.

Be Authentic

We daily encounter multiple opportunities to share the gospel, whether on a plane, eating at a restaurant or shopping in a mall. Ray Comfort's "R.C.C.R." method may come in handy here: "Relate. Create. Convict. Reveal." Begin by being relatable; setting the person at ease; finding some common ground with the person you are talking to. Next, create a way to start talking about God, eternity, the afterlife, etc. Remember to be sensitive to the Holy Spirit, listening for His guidance as He brings the conviction of sin and separation from God. In other words, *a person must realize they are lost, before they can be found.* Before you reveal the solution, make sure the person comprehends that they are lost, separated from God by their sin, and in need of a Savior.

Most people like to talk about their life and what makes them tick, so after breaking the ice and finding common ground, lead up to questions such as, "Do you consider yourself a spiritual person? Or "What do you think your purpose in life is?" This gives you a chance to listen, show genuine concern as they answer, be authentic and ask sincere questions. With this approach you will be able to get a conversation started with just about anyone.

Make sure you ask and remember their name. Someone once told me, There are two things people love to hear: their name and their own opinions. By addressing people by their names, you will be able to build instant rapport with them. And the more you learn about them, the more you will be able to apply the gospel message to their particular situation.

I have found that many people need to improve on their listening skills. It is important to train yourself to listen more than you speak. Good conversations don't begin with proclamations, but rather by meeting people right where they are, asking sincere questions and then really, truly listening. Whenever possible, try to be empathetic. They may have come from a broken, dysfunctional family or had a negative experience with a church or with religion in the past. This will color their understanding of who God is, what the gospel message is about, and even what Christ has done for them.

Empathic listening and the repeated expression of sincere and sympathetic concern on your part can break down many barriers that people might otherwise have. It's not easy to deny the reality of Christ's love when they are being confronted with it.

Establishing authentic relationship is the key to getting the gospel out. Once this rapport is built, the way will be open to bring the subject of mankind's relationship with God into the conversation. Numerous gospel tracts, surveys and Bible studies have been developed to assist in presenting the gospel message (see Appendix).

Keep the Right Attitude

As Christians, it is important to know that the attitude and manner in which we present ourselves can directly influence or hinder others' receptivity to the message we have to share. Although the truth can set you free, it is often difficult to hear. Sometimes we can forget that God is working on our behalf. When confronting people with the truth of the gospel message, we must always remember to couple it with kindness. A haughty, self-righteous attitude will certainly sabotage your message. No matter how another person responds to the truth, we must keep the right attitude.

In the Book of Proverbs it is written:

Do not let kindness and truth leave you; bind them around your neck, write them on the tablet of your heart. So you will find favor and good repute in the sight of God and man.

- Proverbs 3:3-4

Christians are encouraged by Scripture to conduct themselves in a respectful way when interacting with non-believers. Paul instructed the church at Colossae, "Walk in the wisdom of God as you live before the unbelievers, and make it a duty to make Him known. Let every word you speak be drenched with grace and tempered with truth and clarity. For then you will be prepared to give a respectful answer to anyone who asks about your faith" (Colossians 4:5-6 TPT).

Peter encouraged the believers of their day to be armed with both the gospel and with a gentle, understanding spirit. "But sanctify Christ as Lord in your hearts, always being ready to make a defense to everyone who asks you to give an account for the hope that is in you, yet with gentleness and reverence" (1 Peter 3:15). We cannot afford to miss an opportunity to share the good news with another by being condescending, disrespectful or self-righteous toward them. If we hope to influence others towards God, we must aspire to represent Christ to them.

Arguing with an unbeliever will not accomplish anything. You can be right about *what* you are saying, but completely wrong in *how* you are saying it. Even if you answer all of their objections well, and with the right spirit, they may still remain closed to your message. This is why it is important to remember that evangelistic encounters must be undertaken with patience and respect, even toward those who oppose Christ's message.

As Rodney "Gypsy" Smith once said, "There are five Gospels: Matthew, Mark, Luke, John, and the Christian. Most people will never read the first four."[72] In other words, the good news is on display in the person of the Christian who is sharing it, maybe even more than in the content of what he is sharing. When you step out to share the gospel, you put yourself, your character and the name of Jesus on the line with it.

As Paul wrote to advise his young disciple Timothy, we are to correct those in opposition "with gentleness . . . if perhaps God may grant them repentance leading to the knowledge of the truth" (2 Timothy 2:25). Our hope in engaging people with the gospel is that they will come to know Christ and who He is. Remember, very few people will be convinced or attracted to the truth if we present it in an arrogant, quarrelsome way.

The Power of Your Testimony

Come and hear, all who fear God, and I will tell of what He has done for my soul.

- Psalm 66:16

One of the words used for "testimony" in the New Testament is the Greek word *marturia*. It literally means *to provide evidence, to be adduced as a witness.*[73] In other words, what you are about to say or testify of, will provide evidence of something you actually witnessed (experienced) in your life.

Although coming to Christ is a deeply emotional experience, how a person grows in Christ will be greatly affected by how accurate an understanding he has of who Christ is.

> "Tell me your Christology, and I will tell you who you are."
> Our lives will be radically changed or not changed, starting with our decision about who Jesus is. Who we believe Jesus to be determines whether we will allow him to take the central place in our life.
> - Dick Staub[74]

If Jesus is truly God Incarnate, who died on the cross for humanity's sin and rose from the grave on the third day, then miracles are not only possible but, in some cases, inevitable. Our Christian faith is necessarily rooted in real evidence that validates the existence of that faith. Namely, Christians believe God can literally change a human life by extending the grace and forgiveness found in Jesus' atoning death and resurrection.

The Christian's faith is not just a nice personal opinion competing with other religious opinions. We know what we believe and we are convinced that it is true. Knowing and believing the essential truths of God's word are foundational for receiving God's salvation. Scripture clearly teaches us, "Therefore if any man is in Christ, he is a new creature; the old things passed away; behold, new things have come" (2 Corinthians 5:17).

It is understood in Scripture that the gospel is not just the proclamation of the truth but also the demonstration of a changed life produced by the truth. That is why your testimony is so powerful whenever you communicate about your personal experience with God. A transformed life is hard to fake and even harder to dismiss.

People may be excited to talk about what they believe but may not be quite sure how to verbalize it, not being familiar with certain Bible verses or the most theologically accurate way to present what has happened to them. I suggest that believers take the time to write out their personal story of how they came to Christ, in a short, two-minute version, and also in several longer versions, each emphasizing different aspects of their lives, that relate to different audiences. Your testimony should include your recognition that you were lost, separated from God

166

because of your own rebellion, your moment of repentance and full surrender to His loving Lordship, and your growth and experience as a disciple of Christ.

When the realization of God's forgiveness and transforming nature becomes obvious to the believer, the believer's view of the world changes so that it is as if nothing is impossible (Matthew 17:20; 19:26; Mark 10:27; Luke 1:37). The story of this changed life can then impact the most hardened heart with the softening influence of God's power and love.

You may encounter skeptics who will try and dismiss Christianity, Jesus or even religion as a whole, but it is difficult to argue with a changed life. People may attempt to ridicule your faith, but they cannot refute the fact that you and your life have been demonstrably changed.

John encourages Christians that their testimony is key to leading an overcoming life and rising above all the powers of the evil one. He wrote while on the Isle of Patmos: "And they overcame him because of the blood of the Lamb and because of the word of their testimony, and they did not love their life even when faced with death" (Revelation 12:11).

Believers should always be mindful of their main objective: to reach lost people with the gospel. With this in mind, it is important to be ready to share your testimony and tell your story. There is great power in an honest and well-communicated personal testimony.

Address the Problem of Sin

The disease afflicting all unbelievers is that they are alienated from God. The self-centeredness, bondage to sin and feelings of guilt and shame in their lives reveal the emptiness in their hearts that cannot be satisfied except by restoring their relationship with God Almighty. This is true whether they are willing to admit it or not. Saint Augustine wrote of this emptiness in his *Confessions* as follows: "Thou hast made us for thyself, O Lord, and our heart is restless until it finds its rest in thee."[75]

Although some people appear to be happy, carefree or outwardly like they have it all together, inwardly they are plagued by fears, guilt and doubt. The real issue is not that they aren't happy enough, healthy enough, popular enough or rich enough. The real issue is that all people are born "lost" and alienated from God. Man's sinful nature has created a great chasm that separates all of humanity from the presence of a holy and perfect God.

You will find that within a few minutes of conversation, a person will begin to reveal their deepest desires and fears: "For out of the abundance of the heart his mouth speaks" (Luke 6:45 NKJV). Once you've heard what the person is trusting in, you will be able to begin to address the real problem of their sin. As Jesus said, "It is not those who are well who need a physician, but those who are sick" (Luke 5:31). Helping people recognize their need for repentance and reconciliation is the true work of the evangelist.

Unknowingly, people are trying to satisfy this deep longing to know God with cheap counterfeits and substitutes. As a proclaimer of the good news, remember that the real problem people face in life is that they are alienated from the God who made them. Until this spiritual separation is acknowledged and addressed, they will only remain lost and confused.

Don't Chase Rabbits

Staying focused is more difficult today than at perhaps any other time in human history. As a man once said, "When people are trying to take you down a rabbit trail, don't follow them!"

Not only are there personal distractions that try to derail us from engaging others with the gospel, there are also *objections* that people will throw at us when the topic of religion, morality or Christianity comes up. These objections are often quick, superficial responses to Christianity that people have heard before but never taken the time to reason through to their conclusion. These blind attempts to parrot what others have said, are often their last ditch effort to redirect the conversation away from the real issue: *they are beginning to feel the conviction of sin.*

Many objections presented while attempting to engage someone with the gospel will come in the form of questions like: Is there evidence for God's existence? Why is there evil and suffering in the world? Can the Bible really be trusted as God's Word? This makes understanding and using basic apologetics a vital part of the evangelistic task. Recognizing these common arguments and being able to expose the inconsistencies in them, can help the Christian clear away intellectual obstacles to the faith that may be used to distract them while sharing the gospel.

Be aware that many objections to Christianity are not sincere, but serve only to "smokescreen" and divert the conversation away from the gospel presentation. Through practice you will learn how to sidestep these rabbit trails and avoid what can often be pointless philosophical battles meant to suppress the truth.

Scripture tells us that all people are without excuse, aware of

God's existence and attributes through the observation of His creation:

> *For the wrath of God is revealed from heaven against all ungodliness and unrighteousness of men who suppress the truth in unrighteousness, because that which is known about God is evident within them; for God made it evident to them. For since the creation of the world His invisible attributes, His eternal power and divine nature, have been clearly seen, being understood through what has been made, so that they are without excuse.*
>
> - Romans 1:18-20

As you can see, the knowledge of God is not the problem, but a guilty conscious can be. The enemy knows this and manipulates the unbeliever into *suppressing* the truth about God, because they know that they are guilty and their deeds are unrighteous. By denying the truth, the sinner is refusing to acknowledge their own guilt and sin, consequently rejecting the conviction of the Holy Spirit, and denying their need of salvation.

It is paramount that we stay on course and not lose our focus in proclaiming the gospel. Paul boldly declares:

> *For I am not ashamed of the gospel of Christ, for it is the power of God to salvation for everyone who believes, for the Jew first and also for the Greek. For in it the righteousness of God is revealed from faith to faith; as it is written, "The just shall live by faith."*
>
> - Romans 1:16-17 (NKJV)

Remember, it is the gospel that has the power to change people, not our passionate arguments. Center your discussions around the word of God, "For the word of God is living and active and sharper than any two-edged sword, and piercing as far as the division of soul and spirit, of both joints and marrow, and able to judge the thoughts and intentions of the heart" (Hebrews 4:12).

You are not there just to answer their objections to the gospel. Even if you answer all of their objections, God still requires a step of faith to become born again:

> *But what does it say? "The word is near you, in your mouth and in your heart" (that is, the word of faith which we preach): that if you confess with your mouth the Lord Jesus and believe in your heart that God has raised Him from the dead, you will be saved. For with the heart one believes unto righteousness, and with the mouth confession is made unto salvation.*
>
> — Romans 10:8-10 (NKJV)

The questions people ask are important and should be addressed in due course, but do not let these questions dictate the direction of your presentation. Do not be shy about showing someone a verse in the Bible or even asking them to read it to you. It is better that they see first hand that their conflict is with God and not you. You are just the messenger.

Know What You Believe

A preacher once said, "We are not bold in our faith because we do not know what we believe or why we believe it." Unfortunately, many

Christians do not know what they believe, making them hesitant to talk to others about God.

When we engage with people, we want to take them to a place of truth, repentance and ultimately salvation. Whenever attempting to communicate the good news, it's important to remember the essential components of the gospel. At the risk of over-repetition, allow me to reiterate once more what these essentials are. If we try to avoid or change any of these essential elements, our gospel presentation will be inaccurate and ineffective. Let's review the 7 S's:

Sin, Separation, Sacrifice, Substitution, Sorrow, Surrender and Salvation. All people have *sinned* against a holy God who created them. As a result of humanity's choice to sin, all of mankind is justly *separated* from Him, without hope, awaiting judgment. God has lovingly acted in and through the *sacrifice* of His Son, Jesus Christ, offering Him as our sinless *substitute*. By His death on the cross, His burial and His resurrection, Christ redeemed mankind. It is only by the grace of God that man can be granted godly *sorrow* receiving the gift of repentance. It is through placing our faith in what Christ has done for us and by *surrendering* to His Lordship that a person can receive *salvation* and be born-again.

Take Hold of the Truth

Every age and culture has its own challenges for Christian believers to engage their world and be a witness to the life, death, resurrection and transforming power of Jesus Christ. For Christians living in the twenty-first century, even though our task to spread the good news has been made easier by modern technology and air travel that circumnavigates the globe, the job is not finished yet.

The need to engage our world with the gospel is more important now than perhaps at any other time in history. There are cultural philosophies and powers that battle against the ultimate claims of Christianity, but in the end they have nothing to offer in light of the truth. Our present-day politically correct culture has become resistant and hostile toward any message that claims absolute truth, or the idea that absolute truth even exists.

Philosophers like Friedrich Nietzsche conjectured over a century ago what it would be like if God were dead. Since then, many have attempted to behave as though we could manage just fine without God. Consequently, today's believers face the unique challenge of addressing a relativistic, pluralistic cultural mindset rooted in the current world's system of belief that there is no God, and that all that exists is matter, energy, and the undirected physical laws of the universe.

Secularism has mandated political correctness, and multiculturalism has tried to shut down any voice proclaiming to advance one way as superior to all others, yet, such was Jesus' claim: "I am the way, the truth and the life" (John 14:6). We cannot deny or discount who Christ is simply because there are voices in our culture who would prefer for us not to. It is in this chaos of cultural confusion that Christians are meant to be advocates of hope.

You may have arrived at this point and have considered yourself a Christian, not an evangelist. However, the people around you need to hear the gospel message. If you are a true follower of Christ, a real Christian, you will care enough about others to tell them so. "Then

He said to them, 'Follow Me, and I will make you fishers of men.'" (Matthew 4:19). My question to you would be, are you truly following Jesus if you are not participating in reaching the lost in your potential fields of influence? That is why you have been placed where you are placed: "Truly, truly, I say to you, he who believes in Me, the works that I do, he will do also; and greater *works* than these he will do; because I go to the Father" (John 14:12).

This is the eternal truth established before the creation of the world: "For God so loved the world, that He gave His only begotten Son, that whoever believes in Him shall not perish, but have eternal life" (John 3:16). Ignoring God's love-motivated command to share Christ to the lost is refusing to share God's love with others, and, in so doing, refusing to share in it.

You cannot be a true Christian unless you are willing to stand for what Christ stood for, laying down your life and worldly desires in the process: "And He was saying to them *all*, 'If anyone wishes to come after Me, he must deny himself, and take up his cross daily and follow Me'" (Luke 9:23), and, "Whoever does not carry his own cross and come after Me cannot be My disciple" (Luke 4:27).

If we ignore the Great Commission, we also ignore God's enabling strength and power that He has made available to us to accomplish His purpose (Ephesians 3:20). We are without excuse:

> *What then shall we say to these things? If God is for us, who is against us? . . . But in all these things we overwhelmingly conquer through Him who loved us.*
>
> - Romans 8:31, 37

God has placed His resurrection power within us, promised to be with us, given us the promise of His Spirit, and commissioned us to go. Knowing this should give us the courage to overcome all fear and complacency. This perspective should alter the way we approach our lives and the way we interact with those around us. It should motivate us to step out of our comfort zone to broach the subject of God and eternal life with others. It should change the way we interact with those who do not know Christ, who are presently on the road that leads to death and eternal separation from God.

Christ died, for all of mankind. It is our responsibility to present the truth to each giving them the opportunity to receive Him. I believe that God's presence will be with you whenever you testify of His truth and goodness to others.

Final Thoughts

One of our biggest problems is not with the unbelievers we hope to reach with the truth, but with the vast majority of Christian believers who remain silent and apathetic towards the Great Commission. The words of Jesus ring loud and true: "For whoever is ashamed of Me and My words in this adulterous and sinful generation, the Son of Man will also be ashamed of him when He comes in the glory of His Father with the holy angels" (Mark 8:38).

Christianity is an all-encompassing faith. It requires believers to be proactive influencers, real catalysts for cultural change that will take the gospel message wherever they go. A Christianity that mirrors the culture is a Christianity that will become passive and eventually disappear.

The Apostle Paul probably said it best:

But I do not consider my life of any account as dear to myself, so that I may finish my course and the ministry which I received from the Lord Jesus, to testify solemnly of the gospel of the grace of God.

- Acts 20:24

Paul recognized God's agenda to spread the good news as preeminent. This revelation became the primary agenda in Paul's life.

Paul's consuming passion was to testify of the gospel to the rest of the world. To emulate Christ in His earthly ministry is to get serious about doing the "Father's Business" (Luke 2:49).

This obligation to spread the gospel is not just for super-saints like the Apostle Paul, or for pastors, or full-time missionaries. It is for all of us who call upon the name above every name, the name of Jesus. God's divine power is the transforming agent that makes us a new creation in Christ and places upon us, as believers, the ministry of reconciliation. In return, we are intended to be God's ambassadors to the masses of people that have not yet heard or believed in the good news (2 Corinthians 17-18). As the message of grace changes lives, these transformed individuals then become agents of reconciliation.

No loving father would ever give his children a task that was impossible for them to accomplish. Nor does God expect Christians to take the good news to the world without His supernatural aid. God has not left the monumental task of world evangelization to the Christian only; He has graciously sent the Holy Spirit to be present with us and to anoint us for this engagement with the world. Jesus' own words

176

guarantee that He would send us the "Helper" to lead us in the truth and that we would receive power when the Holy Spirit came upon us (John 14:16-17; Acts 1:8).

The promise of the Holy Spirit's presence is not just to comfort the believer, but also to empower the Christian to be a witness wherever he or she may be (Acts 1:8). We can have absolute confidence in the power of the gospel message and in the anointing that rests on being an obedient witness to the truth. God always equips for a specific purpose.

To step outside of our comfort zones and begin to engage the culture is where the real action is. Helen Keller, who was deaf and blind, once said, "Life is either a daring adventure or nothing."[76] I believe the essence of that statement applies to our Christian faith. Our Christianity should be a daring walk of faith engaging our culture with God's eternal truth, or it is worth nothing at all.

Remember to live by the *Rules of Engagement:* 1) Accept Your Mission; 2) Clarify Your Message; 3) Live Your Message; 4) Speak with Confidence; and 5) Think and Act Strategically. Now more than ever we have every opportunity to preach God's truth. My sincere prayer for every person who reads this book is that sharing the good news will no longer be optional.

> *Now to Him who is able to do far more abundantly beyond all that we ask or think, according to the power that works within us, to Him be the glory in the church and in Christ Jesus to all generations forever and ever. Amen.*
>
> - Ephesians 3:20-21

APPENDIX

Additional Tools for Sharing the Gospel

There are many effective resources and evangelistic tools that can be employed to reach out to unbelievers. The idea when initiating contact with someone is to open up the conversation with sincere concern and interest, hearing what they have to say before you administer the witnessing tool, with their permission.

No matter what approach or combination of approaches you take, remember the purpose of why you are doing what you are doing. It's not so much about the technique that you use as about the lives that you are reaching and what God is doing in and through you. The Holy Spirit is able to translate your obedience to follow Him and make disciples of Christ into one of the most rewarding adventures of your life.

I have listed a few additional evangelistic tools that can be utilized to help engage people wherever you find yourself, whether meeting someone for the first time, or with someone you have known for a while.

1. The S.A.L.T. Method:

Dr. Rice Broocks and others like the Fellowship of Christian Athletes (FCA) and The Navigators have used the acronym known as S.A.L.T. as a method to help engage people with the gospel message.

S - Start a conversation,

A - Ask questions,

L - Listen, and

T - Tell the story.[77]

The *story* of course, is some version of your personal testimony and how you came to know Christ. At this point you ask the person, "Have you ever explored what the Bible says about these questions?" Once you get permission from the person, then you can present the gospel to them or set up a time to do so. Techniques like the SALT method are very useful when attempting to talk to a stranger, friend, or relative about God. Remember, people open up whenever they sense you are sincerely concerned for them and listening to them. But whatever method you use: be sensitive, be flexible, and speak from the heart.

2. TheGodTest.

Dr. Rice Broocks has developed an effective evangelism tool called *TheGodTest* (www.thegodtest.org), which I have used around the world and highly recommend. The tool is available in booklet form or as a free download on an app. It helps facilitate discussion on critical issues of faith, skepticism, and the meaning of life. *TheGodTest* is designed to be used in one-on-one or small group discussions, however, it has also been used in settings with larger audiences.

Essentially, *TheGodTest* is not designed as a tract to hand out or as an outline for a mini-lecture to deliver to a captive audience. It is designed to generate conversations about God, and is a dialogical tool.[78]

The central question is: *Do you believe in God?* What follows are a series of questions for those who believe in God (side B), and another for those who consider themselves to be atheists or agnostics (side A). *TheGodTest* is a practical tool for engaging someone in conversation about belief in God. At the end of the app. Dr. Broocks has included a presentation of the gospel for those who would like to continue the discussion.

3. The One 2 One Booklet[79] for Personal Follow-up and Discipleship.

This is an easy-to-use booklet, developed by Steve Murrell, and is ideal for sharing the gospel and for starting to establish new believers into the faith. Its six chapters contain the basic doctrines essential to the Christian faith in thought and practice covering:

1. **Salvation.**
2. **Lordship.**
3. **Repentance.**
4. **Baptism.**
5. **The Bible and Prayer.**
6. **The Church.**

4. The Purple Book: Biblical Foundations for Building Strong Disciples.

The Purple Book is a twelve-chapter comprehensive study of the Bible that is geared at laying biblical foundations in the Christian believer.

The Purple Book is a more thorough Bible study that will help produce scriptural understanding, discipleship and Christian character and can be done individually, or as a small group.[80]

5. The Way of the Master Evangelism Material: Ray Comfort Living Waters Ministries.

Living Waters Ministries has inspired and equipped many for the work of the evangelist. *The Way of Master* by Ray Comfort is an excellent training series that I have used, along with many of their unique witnessing tracts. They also offer an online School of Biblical Evangelism. Their website is: www.livingwaters.com/evangelism.

6. Cru Ministry Gospel Tools.

Cru was originally founded as Campus Crusade for Christ in 1951, when Bill and Vonette Bright began the ministry on the UCLA campus. God had given Bill a vision portraying the total fulfillment of the Great Commission throughout the world. Some Cru Evangelistic Tracts and Tools include: *The Four*, formerly known as the Four Spiritual Laws, God Tool, and The *Jesus* Film.[81]

7. Other Gospel Tools.

Over the years I have used other evangelist tools, that have all proven to be effective in various scenarios including: *The Master Plan of Evangelism* by Robert Coleman,[82] *Evangelism Explosion* by Dr. James Kennedy,[83] *The Alpha Course*, started in 1977, by the Reverend Charles Marnham,[84] and The Two-Question Test by Francis Anfuso.[85] Depending upon your context and situation, some of these tools may work better than others.

Remember, it is the truth of the gospel that changes lives. May God bless you and renew you as you participate in the Great Commission.

ENDNOTES

Introduction

1. Ravi Zacharias, *Walking from East to West: God in the Shadows* (Zondervan, 2009), 178.

2. Jacques Barzun, *From Dawn to Decadence* (New York: HarperCollins, 2000), 26.

3. Ralph Earle, *Word Meanings in the New Testament*, Vol. 1 (Lansing, MI: Baker Books, 1986), 455.

4. Geoffrey W. Bromiley, ed., *The International Standard Bible Encyclopedia*, Vol. 3 (Grand Rapids, MI: Eerdman Publishing Company, 1986), 942.

Chapter One

5. "Rules of Engagement," Britannica.com. Accessed May 12, 2018. Available at: https://www.britannica.com/topic/rules-of-engagement-military-directives.

6. Interview with Jeff Bramstedt, U.S. Navy SEAL (Ret.), 9 April 2015.

7. Engage, Noah Webster, *An American Dictionary of the English Language* (Printed by Hezekiah Howe, 1828).

8. Theologians refer to this concept as the Imago Dei.

Chapter Two

9. "Agenda," definitions 1.1 and 1.2, OxfordDictionaries.com. Accessed May 12, 2018. Available at: https://en.oxforddictionaries.com/definition/agenda.

10. Tullian Tchividjian, *Unfashionable: Making a Difference in the World by Being Different* (New York, NY: Doubleday Religious Publishing Group, 2012), 81.

11. Calvin Miller, *The Vanishing Evangelical: Saving the Church from Its Own Success by Restoring What Really Matters* (Grand Rapids, MI: Baker Books, 2013), 73.

12. Charles Haddon Spurgeon, GoodReads.com. Accessed May 12, 2018. Available at: https://www.goodreads.com/quotes/419253-we-are-not-responsible-to-God-for-the-soul-that.

13. Manfred Brauch, F. F. Bruce, Peter Davids and Walter Kaiser, *Hard Sayings of the Bible* (Downer Gove, IL: Intervarsity Press, 1996), 148.

14. Robert H. Gundry, *A Survey of the New Testament* (Grand Rapids, MI: Zondervan, 1994), 360-61.

15. Ralph Earle, *Word Meaning in the N.T.* Vol. 1 (Lansing, MI: Baker Books, 1994), 135.

16. Os Guinness, *Fit Bodies Fat Minds: Why Evangelicals Don't Think and What to Do About It* (Lansing, MI: Baker Books, 1994), 148.

17. "Confidence," definitions 1 and 1.1. OxfordDictionaries.com. Accessed May 12, 2018. Available at: https://en.oxforddictionaries.com/definition/confidence.

18. In fact, some scholars believe that it was Paul's imprisonment that placed him at the perfect, strategic crossroads to share the gospel with Caesar's Imperial Guard and the servants of the palace. By these means, Christianity found its way into even the most elite Roman circles, and God used even the most unlikely circumstances to make His gospel known.

19. Ralph Earle, *Word Meanings in the New Testament*, Vol. 1 (Lansing, MI: Baker Books, 1986), 208.

20. Russell D. Moore, *Onward: Engaging the Culture without Losing the Gospel* (Nashville, TN: B&H Publishing Group, 2015), 88.

21. Walter A. Elwell, ed., *Evangelical Dictionary of Theology* (Lansing, MI: Baker Books, 1984), 271-72.

22. C. S. Lewis, *Mere Christianity* (New York, NY: HarperCollins, [1952] 2001), 64.

Chapter Three

23. Chan Kilgore, InsightToday.com. Accessed May 12, 2018. Available at: https://insighttoday.com/tag/faith/.

24. Tim Dowley, ed., *The History of Christianity. A Lion Handbook* (Oxford, England: Lion Publishing, 1997), 79, 80.

25. Ralph Earle, *Word Meanings in the New Testament*, Vol. 1 (Lansing, MI: Baker Books, 1986), 111.

26. Of course, the answer in this piece of fiction and film was not 74, but 42. But this serves the point for the purpose of making the illustration.

27. Ralph Earle, *Word Meanings in the New Testament*, Vol. 1 (Lansing, MI: Baker Books, 1986), 313.

28. "Substitution," Definition 2, *Merriam Webster's Collegiate Dictionary*, Eleventh Edition (Springfield, MA: Merriam-Webster, Incorporated, 2007), 1246.

29. Rich Renner, *Sparkling Gems from the Greek*, Vol. 2 (Tulsa, OK: Institute Books, 2016), 203.

30. "Surrender," *English Oxford Living Dictionary*. Accessed September 23, 2017. Available at: https://en.oxforddictionaries.com/definition/surrender.

31. Walter A. Elwell, ed., *Evangelical Dictionary of Theology* (Lansing, MI: Baker Books, 1984), 967.

32. Ibid., 472.

33. Tim Keller, *Christianity Today*, March 7, 2008.

34. Rice Broocks, *TheGodTest: A Study Guide* (2010), 6. Available at: http://www.thegodtest.org.

35. David Platt, *Counter Culture: A Compassionate Call to Counter Culture in a World of Poverty, Same-Sex Marriage, Racism, Sex Slavery, Immigration, Abortion, Persecution, Orphans and Pornography* (Carol Stream, IL: Tyndale House, 2015), 8.

36. Os Guinness, *Fool's Talk: Recovering the Art of Christian Persuasion* (Downers Grove, IL: InterVarsity Press, 2015), 16.

Chapter Four

37. C. S. Lewis, *Mere Christianity* (New York: HarperCollins, 2001), 216.

38. Ralph Earle, *Word Meanings in the New Testament,* Vol. 1 (Lansing, MI: Baker Books, 1986), 199.

39. At the time, he was running on the platform for the Labor Party, who were opposed to family-centric values like the right to life of the unborn.

40. Dallas Willard, *Knowing Christ Today: Why We Can Trust Spiritual Knowledge* (New York, NY: HarperCollins, 2009).

41. Bart Jones, testimony, given, October 1, 2017.

42. Colin Brown, ed., *New International Dictionary of New Testament Theology,* Vol. 3 (Grand Rapids, MI: Zondervan, 1992), 937.

43. James Strong, *The New Strong's Complete Dictionary of Bible Words* (Nashville, TN: Thomas Nelson Publishers, 1996), 201.

44. Norman Geisler and William Nix, *A General Introduction to the Bible* (Chicago: Moody Press, 1980), 116.

45. Os Guinness, *Fool's Talk: Recovering the Art of Christian Persuasion* (Downers Grove, IL: InterVarsity Press, 2015), 119.

46. James McDonald, *When Life is Hard* (Chicago, IL: Moody Publishers, 2010), 136.

47. As David Kinnaman's referenced study also reveals, over 60% of Christians tend to view evangelism as extreme, too: David Kinnaman

and Gabe Lyons, *Good Faith: Being a Christian When Society Thinks You're Irrelevant and Extreme* (Grand Rapids, MI: Baker Books, 2016), 41.

48. Brian K. Morley, *Mapping Apologetics: Comparing Contemporary Approaches* (Grand Rapids, MI: InterVarsity Press, 2015), 35.

49. David Kinnaman and Gabe Lyons, *Good Faith: Being a Christian When Society Thinks You're Irrelevant and Extreme* (Grand Rapids, MI: Baker Books, 2016), 12.

50. ". . . Thy Kingdom come, Thy Will be done, on earth as it is in Heaven. . . ."

51. Calvin Miller, *The Vanishing Evangelical: Saving the Church From its Own Success by Restoring What Really Matters* (Grand Rapids, MI: Baker Books, 2013), 215.

52. C. S. Lewis, *God in the Dock: Essays on Theology and Ethics* (Lansing, MI: Eerdmans, 1972), 101.

53. Nancy Pearcey, *Saving Leonardo* (Nashville, TN: B&H Publishing Group, 2010), 15.

54. Abraham Kuyper, "Sphere Sovereignty," in *Abraham Kuyper: A Centennial Reader*, ed. James D. Bratt (Grand Rapids, MI: Eerdmans, 1988), 461.

Chapter Five

55. R. J. Rushdoony, *A Word in Season*, Vol. 1 (Vallecito, CA: Ross House Books, 2010).

56. James Strong, *The New Strong's Complete Dictionary of Bible Words*

(Nashville, TN: Thomas Nelson Publishers, 1996), 420. See also *Strong's Exhaustive Concordance*, Hebrew 4170. Accessed September 23, 2017. Available at: http://biblehub.com/str/hebrew/4170.htm.

57. "Glossophobia," *Wikipedia*. Accessed September 12, 2017. Available at: https://en.wikipedia.org/wiki/Glossophobia.

58. "Tolerance," Noah Webster, *An American Dictionary of the English Language* (Printed by Hezekiah Howe, 1828).

59. "Tolerance," Definitions 1 and 2a, *Merriam Webster's Collegiate Dictionary*, Eleventh Edition (Springfield, MA: Merriam-Webster, Incorporated, 2007), 1315.

60. David Kinnaman and Gabe Lyons, *Good Faith: Being a Christian When Society Thinks You're Irrelevant and Extreme* (Grand Rapids, MI: Baker Books, 2016), 18.

61. "Forbearance," Definition 3 and 2. Noah Webster, *An American Dictionary of the English Language* (Printed by Hezekiah Howe, 1828).

62. "Sycophant," Noah Webster, An American Dictionary of the English Language (Printed by Hezekiah Howe, 1828).

63. Ralph Earle, *Word Meanings in the New Testament*, Vol. 1 (Lansing, MI: Baker Books, 1986), 311.

Chapter Six

64. In terms of the history of military-jargon, the expression "boots on the ground" dates back at least to British officer Robert Grainger Ker Thompson and is also associated with General William Westmoreland, as per Wikipedia. "Boots on the Ground," *Wikipedia*. Last updated May

30, 2017. Accessed September 28, 2017. Available at: https://en.wikipedia.org/wiki/Boots_on_the_Ground.

65. Alister E. McGrath, *Historical Theology: An Introduction to the History of Christian Thought* (Oxford, UK: Blackwell Publishing, 1998), 249.

66. Christian History. Accessed November 14, 2017. Available at: www.christianitytoday.com/history/people/evangelistsandapologist/dwight-l-moody.

67. Thomas Edison, QuoteInvestigator.com. Accessed May 12, 2018. https://quoteinvestigator.com/2012/08/13/overalls-work/amp/.

68. Tim Elmore, *Habitudes: Images that Form Leadership and Attitudes* (Atlanta, GA: Growing Leaders Inc., 2010), 37.

69. Definition 2b, Thayer's Greek Lexicon, Strong's New Testament 2540. Accessed September 23, 2017. Available at: http://biblehub.com/str/greek/2540.htm. See also at same source: HELPS Word-studies 1987, 2011. Helps Ministries, Inc.

70. Francis A. Schaeffer, *The Christian View of the Church*, 2nd Ed., Vol. 4 (Wheaton, IL: Crossway Books, 1985), 110.

71. Ed Stetzer and Thom Rainer, *Transformational Church* (Nashville, TN: B&H Publishing Group and LifeWay Research, 2010), 66.

Conclusion

72. Rodney "Gipsy" Smith, Azquotes.com. Accessed May 12, 2018. Available at: https://www.azquotes.com/author/50640-Rodney_Gipsy_Smith.

73. James Strong, *The New Strong's Complete Dictionary of Bible Words* (Nashville, TN: Thomas Nelson Publishers, 1996), 655.

74. Dick Staub, *The Culturally Savvy Christian: A Manifesto for Deepening Faith and Enriching Popular Culture in an Age of Christianity-Lite* (San Francisco, CA: John Wiley & Sons, Inc., 2007), 77.

75. Augustine of Hippo, Confessions. Accessed May 12, 2018. Available at: https://www.goodreads.com/work/quotes/1427207.

76. Helen Keller, QuoteInvestigator.com. Accessed May 12, 2018. Available at: https://quoteinvestigator.com/2014/11/21/adventure/amp/.

Appendix

77. Rice Broocks, *TheGodTest Study Guide* (2010). Available for download at: http://www.thegodtest.org.

78. Ibid., 3

79. Steve Murrell, *One 2 One: Personal Follow-up and Discipleship* (Nashville, TN: Every Nation Productions, 1996-2009).

80. Rice Broocks and Steve Murrell, *The Purple Book: Biblical Foundations for Building Strong Disciples* (Grand Rapids, MI: Zondervan Press, 2004).

81. Links to these and other resources are available at: www.cru.org.

82. Robert E. Coleman, *The Master Plan of Evangelism* (Old Tapper, NJ: Fleming H Revell Publishing 1972).

83. James Kennedy, https://www.amazon.com/Evangelism-Explosion-4th-James-Kennedy/dp/0842307648.

84. Charles Marnham, https://www.alphausa.org.

85. Francis Anfuso, http://www.twoquestiontest.com.

About the Author

Ken Dew is a church-planter and equipping evangelist who trains the body of Christ to engage the lost with the gospel. Ken moved with his family from Nashville, Tennessee to Auckland, New Zealand in the year 2000 to begin planting Every Nation Churches in the South Pacific region. During that time he served on the Every Nation International Oversight Team as Regional Director. Ken and his wife Renee have been instrumental in establishing multiple Every Nations Churches in New Zealand, Australia, and the island nation of Fiji. The region continues to grow with new ministries in Canberra, Australia and Papua New Guinea.

A graduate from Tennessee Technological University, Ken also holds a Master of Theology from Luther Rice College and Seminary and a Master of Apologetics, on-going. Ken and his wife currently reside in the Dallas-Fort Worth area, and they have four grown children.

Engaging the Culture:

Why Sharing Your Faith is No Longer an Option
By Ken Dew

More copies available at
www.KenDewResources.com
Also available at bookstores
and as an eBook.

For more information:

Website: www.KenDewResources.com

Twitter: @kendewresources

Email: kendewresources@gmail.com

Ken's next book:

The Certainty of Christ:
Why We Persuade Men

NOTES

NOTES

CPSIA information can be obtained
at www.ICGtesting.com
Printed in the USA
FFHW021805040419
51495402-56953FF